American Developer

American Developer

A Practical Guide to Extending Business Internationally

in a World that Is Flat in Places

by Kevin G. McGibben

iUniverse, Inc.
New York   Bloomington

American Developer
A Practical Guide to Extending Business
Internationally in a World that Is Flat in Places

iUniverse books may be ordered through booksellers or by contacting:

iUniverse
1663 Liberty Drive
Bloomington, IN 47403
www.iuniverse.com
1-800-Authors (1-800-288-4677)

Because of the dynamic nature of the Internet, any Web addresses or links contained in this book may have changed since publication and may no longer be valid. The views expressed in this work are solely those of the author and do not necessarily reflect the views of the publisher, and the publisher hereby disclaims any responsibility for them.

ISBN: 978-1-4401-2742-7 (pbk)
ISBN: 978-1-4401-2744-1 (cloth)
ISBN: 978-1-4401-2743-4 (ebk)

Printed in the United States of America

iUniverse rev. date: 3/10/2009

Contents

Foreword

Kevin McGibben has provided us with a long-needed "how to" book on developing international markets. His book is constructed both from his research and teaching, and from years of developing international markets for his own company and other companies for whom he has consulted. It is targeted to both business professionals that are pursuing international markets as well as graduate business students looking to learn the ropes of international business and marketing.

My perspective on the importance of this book is derived from my work with MBA student teams over the past twenty-five years to provide business plans and launch strategies for companies that want to take their products and services across borders. In general, the MBA teams have provided custom research for their clients because the materials on how to succeed in international markets is scattered, incomplete, and mostly theoretical.

One of the obvious conclusions from spending a quarter century in international business is that the people, products, and approaches that bring success in the domestic market will not necessarily succeed overseas. There are clear reasons for why it makes sense to go international, and improved return on investment is one of them, but short-term financial gain is not. The company needs to be equipped with the capability to enter a new market including expertise and experience, production or service capacity, deep pockets, and commitment to stay the course.

Products need to be adapted or "localized," sometimes to a significant extent. I do not know of a product or service that does not require some type of customization to be sold overseas. This change might be as insignificant as a translated label or different packaging, or as significant as a major change in design or ingredients. The entire production facility may need to be altered to accommodate the changes. The issues in setting up distribution or arranging for warehousing or setting up production facilities in a foreign market are exponentially more difficult than doing so in the domestic market. Provision of services may require significant skill in languages and cultures that are new to the company.

To adapt the product or service successfully, one must understand the foreign market thoroughly and how consumers will respond to your entry. Even if the product is successfully localized, can it compete with existing competitors or substitute products? Can the organization provide the training, support, or service necessary to keep consumers satisfied?

What about getting the product to market or setting up the service organization abroad? There are shipping and supply chain issues to be overcome, regulations to be understood and addressed, and payment and currency issues to be negotiated. International markets are not for the feint of heart and not for businesses lacking the broad scale knowledge and expertise to succeed.

I have been surprised numerous times over the years to observe that well-established American companies are unprepared to enter specific international markets, and that the approach that they have planned to use is destined to fail. I can understand this lack of preparation for a small company that is new to international business, but it is shocking to me when Fortune 500 companies are not sufficiently prepared to succeed.

McGibben's book offers the reader a comprehensive and step-by-step guide on how to conduct the proper exploratory research and how to construct the launch strategy and operations so that a business can start off on the right foot. He then moves into how to develop, grow, and sustain the overseas market. Although reading and absorbing the book's many ideas and insights will not guarantee success for every business, it will certainly help avoid the common mistakes committed by all too many American business ventures.

Ernest J. Scalberg
Associate Vice President for External Programs and
Dean of the Fisher Graduate School of International Business
Monterey Institute of International Studies
Monterey, California

About the Author

An adjunct professor in international marketing, **Kevin McGibben** has extensive experience in implementing international business strategies in emerging markets. He is the founder of the international market development consultancy, 32 South, a business which helps companies expand and implement their businesses internationally. He resides in Santa Cruz, California.

Preface

Why I Wrote This Book

Most business reading material is meant to build your business knowledge from a theoretical basis. Typically, business readings offer ideas about a skill or functional area of business with a fresh perspective, the latest thinking, or a unique approach about a given topic. Examples are the myriad of operational management books or books on various leadership skills. Another variety of business books offers macro overviews presenting a statement on the status of things, such as international business books on what might or might not be "globalization." Very few books are cookbooks (recipes for success) for business functional areas. This book, however, was written to offer you a useable guide on how to assess and implement an international business effort.

When I finished my undergraduate degree in history at the University of Arizona, I clearly recall wondering whether I could parlay my Latin American history and Spanish education into a career. Unlike most post-MBA careers, jumping into international business doesn't have a formalized career path. There usually are only a limited number of entry-level positions focused on international business, since typically firms want seasoned professionals who have some international experience to be involved in their international efforts. Occasionally, firms will hire directly into an international role, but typically those limited positions require previous work experience or graduation from a top-tier MBA program.

Reading this book does not guarantee success in international business, but it will serve as a guide to many fundamental issues and principles that, managed properly, might save your job. I learned this knowledge largely by personal experience. Sure, I went to business school, studied international marketing, and over the years have kept up on the marketing advances in international strategy thinking (which has not changed dramatically in the past fifteen years). American "B school" business students are not taught all of the skills required to succeed in international business. I suppose this is because many of these skills are not considered practical, and thus the skills that are deemed more practical and important are given more thorough treatment in order for students to leverage those skills into business success. As a result, there are many people interested in international business, students and established businesspeople alike, who do not have a complete understanding of what their potential ideal career choice may actually require in order to succeed.

Why This Book Is Unique

The definition of international business can be wide-ranging and ambiguous. In this book, I focus on developing international business for the organization that is without a significant, established recipe for international expansion. In other words, this is not a book to tell Citibank how to offer yet another branch office like the other thousands they have around the world. My focus is for the clothier, the software firm, the technology company, the consumer electronics manufacturer, the farmer, the vintner, and the industrial products company trying to determine whether to expand business internationally. Specifically, this book is for anyone or any group, in any size company, who is going into uncharted territory and new markets, whether "developing" economies or not.

What You Can Gain Reading This Book

Are you interested in making international business (marketing, sales, product development, management, finance, operations) your career? Is your organization struggling with current international start-up issues? Do you have new management responsibility, and international business is new to you? This book should be a big help. If you are wondering whether your organization should be considering international markets as a way to grow your business, you are not alone. As I'll discuss later, international market development—or expansion of business into new international markets—is driven by virtually any functional area within a company. If you are in a position of responsibility for your firm's international growth, do you have any idea what issues you should consider in order to be able to make development and management decisions?

Perhaps you are an expatriate (someone who is a foreign citizen working internationally) working in an international assignment who wants to know the typical risks, impedances, pitfalls, and keys to success in implementing an international approach to your current business. I may not answer all of your questions, but this book addresses a lot of them and will answer many. I am confident my real-life struggles, education, and successes, which I share with you in this book, can provide insight and be helpful in getting you started to find your own answers.

Regardless of your formal education and where it was received, the plain truth of the matter is that to succeed in development of new international business, you need a mix of personal skills, education, and organizational resources. Some of you may be asking yourself, "Do I need an MBA to conduct and lead international business?" Unless you are a crusader within a small business or a high-level sales or marketing executive in an expanding business, the only explicit advantage you will get from an MBA is that it will be easier for you to get your foot in the proverbial international door. This is a fact of North American business. And although students can waste time in an MBA program as well as in any other, generally speaking, MBA programs prepare a student well for the international business field due to the general familiarity the students have with most aspects of business. Rather than be too worried about what you might or might not learn by entering an MBA program, take some solace in this: regardless of whether they have advanced degrees, the successful international development people I have met share many of the characteristics described in this book.

My sincere hope is that through this book, I can share insights that might make your job and career a little easier than the road I've hoed.

Experience Is the Best Teacher

I have drawn upon my personal experiences and knowledge of the fundamentals of international marketing to create a book that is a working text for how to implement international business development strategies for your organization. Along the way, I'll point out the issues you surely will confront on your path toward taking your business international. My career has spanned several high and low technology areas in the modern economy. Even though I don't have direct experience in agriculture, textiles, mining, hospitality, or heavy manufacturing, for example, the people with whom I have discussed international market development strategy who do know those fields agree that the same issues impact international market development across industries. The firms I have worked with over the years generally offer new or successful technology products (that in turn enable new services) in markets where such products or services would not have been considered fifteen years ago.

After receiving a master of business administration (MBA) degree in marketing (with an international marketing focus) in the first half of the 1990s, I quickly realized no one wanted to hire a fresh MBA for any international positions already established in a firm. It was a time when world markets were opening to the United States—the Cold War had ended only a few years earlier, democracies were taking hold in South America after decades of military rule, and the North American Free Trade Agreement (NAFTA) was in its first year of implementation. So, as many fresh MBA graduates have done, I landed a marketing product management job with a Japanese high-technology company.

I quickly learned the product management job I was hired for and within a short time began talking to my mentor about international opportunities. He was gracious enough to ask his management peers if there were any open internationally focused positions within the organization. It turned out that three months later, a current executive was to receive the reigns of a new international division to manage the Americas from our U.S. office. The person selected for the job spoke little Spanish but had a great deal of experience in U.S.-centric business, so I jumped at my opportunity. I asked my current boss for permission to approach the "international heir" to evaluate potential opportunities. He granted me permission, but when I spoke with the new international executive, he saw no need to staff the new division with additional employees ("we're just going to start distribution in Mexico, that's all," he said). I took some time to research my graduate work and presented a case to the new division manager, describing what he should consider when creating his own business strategy. My ideas included properly evaluating the Americas' market potential for our products, defining resource requirements, and setting forecasts for growth to the company's directors, including the Japanese ownership. Being an opportunist, he jumped at the offer for the pro bono assistance. Three months later, after countless long nights and weekends creating Fujistu's business plan for tackling the Americas, I landed my second job.

I toiled for the first six months; they were full of late nights searching library records (this was the year before the Internet became a useful tool to American business), reading data research texts about Latin America, and creating business plans. Because of my experience in graduate school, I was prepared to organize a research effort necessary to investigate and evaluate any business opportunity. The research and planning I did resulted in my first permanent international position as an international marketing manager. My specific role was to establish the business entry strategy for our American subsidiary of a Japanese conglomerate that had once tried and failed in the same American markets. The reasons for the Japanese failure in the American markets will be easy to recognize for those who finish reading this book and those who understand traditional Japanese *keiretsu* distribution methods.

Unfortunately for the company (but good for my experience), our ability to succeed was arbitrarily constrained by the territory, product mix, and distribution models mandated by the Japanese ownership. The best example of the challenges imposed on us was when the Japanese management ordered us to remove the Brazilian market from any new distribution consideration since the Japanese had "failed miserably" attempting to enter the Brazilian market. If I'd had the practical experience or the perspective I have today, including much of what is written in this book, I would have been able to explain to the Japanese why they failed and what they could do differently the second time around. Eventually our experience in Mexico and the Caribbean led to limited success, but our opportunities were diminished due to poor decision-making on the U.S. executive side. To be fair, the international strategy was very narrowly focused, and the company did not buy in to the shifts needed in the marketing mix and distribution strategy in order to be a huge success. The decisions we made based on the parameters we were dealt did serve me down the road in preparing me well for my own later responsibilities in managing international business development in the Latin America and other emerging markets.

For my second stint in international marketing I followed a former Fujitsu executive to another firm to manage an inherited distribution network for what they called "ROW" (rest of world: Latin America, Oceania, Africa, and parts of Eastern Europe and the Middle East). In the mid-1990s, ROW was the part of the world no one else wanted to manage, but it was right up my alley. The experience was great, although the indirect distribution network I inherited was mostly bad, and the job was essentially a clean-up operation. The firm I worked for, Tekelec, had an established global business—primarily indirect distribution—in multiple product divisions. My area of responsibility overlapped with other product division managers running around managing indirect distribution in some of the same markets.

The distributors I inherited in Israel, Brazil, Chile, Australia, Peru, and South Africa had problems of one level or another, and most of them needed to be replaced by new distributors. The markets where the distributor was solid (Mexico, Argentina, and Venezuela) did not provide the company much business opportunity.

These two experiences solidified my understanding of developing global business and later my creation of a new theory behind the importance of the prioritization of markets. The concept of spending resources strategically such that focus is placed in markets where a good return on investment is likely, given all of the internationalization parameters (change in marketing mix; cultural, business, and political issues; currency fluctuations; and others) and related expenditures, is a relatively novel concept and is presented in this book.

Another variable that heightened my own professional challenges was that both of the companies I had first worked with had product strategies that were not necessarily a good fit for the markets in which I was to focus my development efforts. Again, this was not fully understood initially but realized as a result of my work to assess the markets. Previous executive and regional managers should have chosen a better international development strategy and should have been more discerning in choosing channel partners. My experience in channel management informs much of the insight provided in this text.

In the third corporation I worked for, I was responsible for developing relationships with those companies that were our primary technology service providers, first in Latin America and then worldwide, to expand the company's successful U.S. and Asian business to "virgin" markets. Though the company had some limited entry into Latin America and the rest of the world, which included owning a European subsidiary that was later spun off and then reacquired, I essentially built out a fledgling international business into something significant. I entered the international market with a functional and applicable product (albeit a premium product that was high-priced for emerging markets), along with a relatively strong U.S. market position. These two benefits, a viable product and a strong home-market position, provided a solid opportunity to apply my skills to a more successful international venture.

Looking back on the success, a good amount of it can be attributed to the long-term, in-country relationships and specific market knowledge that had been developed over several years prior to taking on this position. In addition to the in-country understanding, I'd used significant planning and strategic management techniques as generally described in this book to manage the business successfully. Planning, market knowledge, channel development strategies, and managing the expectations back home while advocating the customer or market position all contributed to a successful experience.

In late 2001, shortly after 9/11, I decided to leave my employment for my own international venture in starting up McGibben International (MI). MI was founded originally as an international market development firm and was created to provide strategic planning and even channel development or sales representation for technology companies in the Americas and possibly Europe. I'd determined that my relationships in the Americas and in the European Union (EU) were strong enough to bring new business ideas to them. The first six months played out as expected, where I had a few customers who had contracted for various strategic planning and market representation, but I realized that MI acting as a direct vendor to the market niches where I'd worked previously would generate more revenue and contribution margin. MI ended up continuing to manage much of my previous firm's business, and over time those accounts were transitioned to MI directly.

From there, MI identified product niche opportunities and created a network of in-country partnerships. MI also created a product development methodology and developed relationships with contract manufacturers in Asia that turned out to be quite successful for MI. Of course, MI had endured its share of ups and downs to provide more learning opportunities. MI competes head on with companies like Thompson, Siemens, and lesser-known Chinese manufacturers for telecom operators' Customer Premise Equipment, or "CPE," business as a direct vendor. The Chinese entry and domination of the consumer electronics space is worthy of significant discussion in its own right, but we'll accept it as a fact and not provide it treatment in this text so that we don't go off topic in this book. And although maintaining a constant strategic view of the business is a significant challenge and tends to ebb and flow due to the requirement to bring in cash flow, MI's initial success, especially in light of the commoditization of the product portfolio over time, was due again to the same business principals defined in this book.

Along the way I have had occasional opportunities to dabble in other international ventures. For example, in 2004 and 2005, I cofounded and entered into a venture where a business mentor of mine and I partnered with a publicly traded Asian firm to purchase an operators license in Argentina to offer telephone services using a technology based on Internet telephony (i.e., voice over Internet protocol, or VOIP) services. Ultimately, that business failed to get off the ground to the point that it was self-sustaining, so we pulled out of it, spinning it off to the local in-country partner. I will use some of the experiences learned during that effort to expound on some of the topics discussed later.

In 2005 I began working as a seminar instructor for the Fisher Business School at the Monterey Institute of International Studies in Monterey, California. Teaching MBA students about the realities of implementing international strategy has been a rewarding effort. I recall wondering during my own school years why more practical experience wasn't introduced into the curriculum. Several times over the years, when learning a hard lesson about international business, I remember thinking *I never learned that in school!*

In 2007 I realized that my original concept for MI, to assist companies trying to extend their business model into emerging markets, had some merit. A handful of companies over the years had asked me for advice regarding their market entry and development strategy. I have never been one to hold back an opinion when asked. So, we created a new arm of our business called 32 South as an international market development firm. Over the past year and a half, we've helped several companies that were successful in their home markets to expand internationally. The strategies we formulate to help clients extend their business are the same discussed in these pages. In fact, the past twelve months of work strengthened my resolve to complete this book to help other business people find their way in global markets.

My most recent venture began in 2007, when I was approached by an old business associate and assisted to put together the founding of PrimeTel, a licensed telecommunications (VOIP based) service provider in South Africa. I spearheaded putting together the investment group and act as an advisor to the board for the company. PrimeTel was able to secure a telecommunications service provider license in South Africa, and successfully launched services in Johannesburg in June of 2008. PrimeTel is continuing to add new and exciting services to its business, and the board of directors is focused on building a successful South African business. Of course, I personally hope to see expansion of PrimeTel into Pan-African and possibly other similar international markets.

Introduction

"Dale (da-le)," she said, after I pulled the beer across the chipped mahogany bar in front of me. Her eyes were mirrored reflections of the dark Irish stout in her glass. "Shoo haben't veeseeted Iguazú (ē-guâsu)?" asked the incredulous dark-haired woman in her broken English. I knew she referred to the famous waterfalls located at the intersection of the northeastern border where Argentina sneaks up in between Brazil and Paraguay. Perhaps the world's most dramatic water falls, the disputed region provides oxygen to the fire of Brazil and Argentina's love-hate relationship.

"No, not yet, but I hope I can see them in the near future," was my deadpan Castilian reply. My response was subtle but appropriately respectful of Argentina's natural splendor. The waiter shimmied by behind her, his shoulder-length hair brushing along her back between the spaghetti straps of her short summer dress.

The bar was getting louder and darker as the night disappeared, but the Kilkenny, I had learned over time, would thrive until the wee hours of the morning. Heavy bands of white-gray smoke swirled across the room, riding the waves of forced air drafts, settling the wet chocolate smell of Cuban cigars into all corners of the pub. The Porteña beauty and I settled into deep conversation now, ignoring the wailing of the twenty-something band singer belting out another rendition of a U2 *Joshua Tree* track. During our conversation, we were switching in and out of English and Castilian (Argentine Spanish, castellano, not to be confused with the Spanish of the Castilians spoken in Madrid), she breathily working the former, and I easily working the latter. Though I strained to filter her words into familiar phrases, she was quite fluent when she finally swept the dark strands to reveal her eyes and said, "Do shoo want to go ssommplece else for sum shampen?" My hearing sharpened, and I nodded my approval to the beautiful, strong-featured Argentine face.

We struggled through the crowd clanging through the double

doors in the smoky entry hall, and the outer doors squeaked heavily as we shuffled out into the cold Buenos Aires night. Quickly ducking into the waiting yellow and black Peugeot, the slender figure next to me slipped her hand into mine and demanded the driver to deliver us to the Café Central down in Palermo. (Buenos Aires has two Italian neighborhoods—Palermo, home of the great central park of the same name, and Belgrano, the fashionable high-rent district for the young married (or otherwise rebellious) professionals who no longer live at home with their parents.)

We pulled into the Palermo neighborhood, and to the left about three blocks out I noted the familiar Café Central neon sign hanging from the façade that claimed it as the only all-nighter café in the city. Other than the more classic restaurants of the Palermo area, Buenos Aires struggles with classic haunts advertised in American style. That the café advertises its hours is for the newcomer; every reputable nightspot with hangers-on within four thousand miles remains open until the last person leaves. We gained speed for the final two blocks, zipping through the rain-stained streets at high speed. The smell of fresh rain tinged with diesel permeated the air. Porteño taxi drivers took advantage of empty streets when they had the rare occasion to drive them. Squealing into a U-turn and jerking the car to a halt against the low curb, the driver motioned with his right side to the café door.

I had no small bills on me as usual. With no *monedas* as proper change, the driver scoffed and scowled and drove off hastily in search of another fare as soon as we exited the cab. Like most Buenos Aires taxi drivers, he chose to not get paid rather than to stoop to making change, or, even worse, ask for money from a beautiful Argentine lady (Argentine women will vehemently deny this, but I have seen it happen a handful of times). Who am I to step in the way of ingrained culture and insist to the man? Stepping onto the curb I made a mental note to continue my habit of never carrying coins with me while in Buenos Aires.

The huge wooden door swung open to reveal darkness, interrupted by the occasional candlelight. Small groups of votive candles marked the dozen tightly spaced iron tables. With a nod from the hostess stuck in deep conversation with the barman while seated at the high-stooled, brass-railed mahogany bar across the room, we pointed ourselves clumsily to a corner table looking back out onto the lit street corner. The lady ordered champagne for the both of us and watched intently as a waiter smashed it into a large black ceramic jug filled with fruit. We filled champagne glasses and drank quickly without conversation. With a nod from my beautiful companion, I refilled the glasses, and the champagne level continued to drop in each glass.

Suddenly her English improved—or my hearing failed—as the pitcher emptied, her eyes looking through me with each word. Everyone in Argentina has a way of looking directly into your eyes in a way that makes you feel you are the most interesting thing since sliced bread. Tilting the base of the glass parallel with the ceiling, I finished off the fruit chunks and announced a call to the night. Not to be deterred, the young lady rifled off a question, now using her native tongue for the effect of stating it as a command. "Do you want to kiss me?" As we pushed ourselves away from the table, she let slip the more telling offer to take me by the Plaza, because it wasn't an inconvenience. I would learn later that morning she lived in her family home just northwest of the city in the popular suburb of San Ysidro—the exact opposite direction from the lush, purple-flowered trees of the Plaza San Martin and its famous hotel.

--

The next morning was the first day of my eleventh trip to the city of good air. I pulled myself out of bed at 9:00 a.m. and cursed the time difference from far-off California. I clumsily picked up the telephone and urged the room service staff to bring my coffee and a newspaper ("immediately, sir"). Thirty-five minutes later, the coffee arrived, and I stepped out onto the patio, swallowing hard to get the strong brew down. The breeze was kicking whitecaps up on the brown river in the near distance, offering a stark contrast to the purple-blossoming treetops covering the plaza and extending out toward the river Plate. A half hour later I stepped out onto the street below. The wind was gusting so strongly that when I opened my mouth, it stung the back of my throat. Clouds of exhaust were swept by to stain my suit, and I was reminded that regardless of where you were in the world—particularly South America—or how you translate the words from the native tongue into English, the place names rarely fit the actual place.

I hailed a cab, and we rolled slowly through the streets. It was a short trip down from the Plaza Hotel, passing back past the Kilkenny as the loose newspaper pages flung themselves wildly around the streets, pelting pedestrian commuters inching their way in the throngs toward our destination of Puerto Madero. Setting out toward the brown river, the refurbished dark brick port warehouse building was now the customer's secret paradise. I arrived for my morning meeting feeling good about the country (a state of being familiar to seasoned travelers—one where you have a physically satisfied sensation brought on by the fact you are standing, or sitting, or eating wherever it may be on this small planet). I ducked out of the cab into a fierce morning wind and was presented with a colder than normal Buenos Aires June day.

I entered the posh corporate offices through the side door, passing the pistol-toting security guard who leaned lazily against the reception counter. Surely the corporate heads in Europe who knew about the site in Puerto Madero laughed or scowled each time they thought about the "country site" when seated in a dreary, gray office in Madrid.

The woman at the lobby reception desk gave me a familiar nod. "Señor Macgeeben, how are you?" The Argentine capacity for remembering names is intimidating. Grabbing my security credential, I returned the nod, then turned to head toward the elevators, where the elevator host greeted me with a bulge in his coat in the vicinity of his rib cage. I shook hands and was hurried to the top floor.

Upon arrival at the ante-office, I spent a moment exchanging salutations with Miguel's cropped-red-hair assistant, Victoria. Victoria's husband and I play golf with Miguel on occasion when passing through the country. She led me to Miguel's office. I opened the door, and I was hit by the familiar smell of day-old Cuban cigars lightly lingering about the leather furniture. In front was the always spectacular view of the River Plate and its chocolate waves whipping small sailboats around like toys in a bathtub. The masts of the larger boats just below the window of this office could punch through the window at any moment to interrupt our meeting. Miguel immediately stood and passed his underlings as though they were furniture, offering me his hand and the traditional kiss on the right cheek that is so common among Argentine friends. This traditional greeting is common among good friends in

Argentina, but a rarity in business circles. I always greet Miguel this way, especially when his underlings are present as a reminded to them of my potential influence and mandated acceptance in the group.

I eventually sat down in the corner seat in which Miguel directed me to sit from behind his oversized desk, without a word, and with a dramatic sweep of his arm; the corner seat faced the others, not the view. The better to make sure I felt the eyes in the room. The meeting would be choreographed, beginning with the initial interruption of Victoria's entrance in a short skirt to take coffee orders from the seated party. As I settled in to the soft leather seat, Victoria returned with what was probably French coffee after Miguel mumbled something into the desktop telephone speaker from his desk on the south side of the giant office. It was then that I made the necessary introductions to the new faces in the group in front of me. Each time a major negotiation is about to take place, new actors join in to provide a balance of the unknown and untested to leverage the side of the locals. These new actors really didn't matter much, however, to the business at hand.

Miguel stood, set both hands flat on his desk, palms flush. He then slightly bowed to acknowledge the others as he took his seat at the head of the group. He started, "I am sorry, but we cannot complete this deal with its current structure." I knew from experience that because he passed the usually genuine and lengthy pleasantries that the audience in the room had a clear agenda and that these people would not be wasting their time to simply play host to a Yankee like me and then go on to terminate our negotiations for a major pending contract.

I played along, posturing by squirming a bit in my seat. "But Miguel, we have been through the proposal, and surely you know the wall I am up against. I have done all that is possible to do."

Miguel replied, "You must understand, in order to be able to go forward, it is we who will make the decision [a power play noting our perimeter negotiations with his global purchasing group in Europe], and we haven't received the right offer to present the business justification to the board." I think he knew I had studied well. Miguel had decision authority for the subsidiary—with approval from the executives in Europe—and any reference to the board was a show, and he had to know I knew it. He was doing a song and dance for the group in the room to remind them of the pecking order. Miguel and I had shared numerous bottles of Argentine red wine and French champagne at the finer Puerto Madero establishments.

He continued, "In a good faith effort to move forward, I'd like to offer the following counterproposal to what we have discussed." If the deal changed once it changed twenty times, more often as the close neared. I had arrived prepared and ready to provide another token gesture in hopes to secure the contract, and so I did. He smiled in reaction to my response, and the other members of the group gave him deft looks of serious approval. It was over. Hands were shaken, and the final details would be negotiated later. I headed out the door and looked forward to sharing the news with management back in Silicon Valley.

--

Four years of work paid off in my first sizable international contract, confirmed a week after the Puerto Madero meeting with a phone call. One of the Spaniards caught me while I was tying a prince nymph on my leader line in preparation to catch rainbow trout on the Merced River in northern California, just west of Yosemite. But it was leaving Miguel's water-front office building that afternoon a week earlier, after a full lunch of champagne, filet mignon, and dry red wine when I realized I knew the process it took to really get business started and closed outside the United States. I decided to start writing things down.

1

Getting Started in International Business

Somewhere over the north end of the Andes range I said a silent prayer for the plane to run into the nearest mountaintop to take me out of my misery. The Brazilians and their wicked *cachaça* were to blame. After seven hours in coach, my legs were cramping, the pangs exacerbated by the fact that I hadn't slept in a day and a half. My head felt like it was going to explode from the combination of the *cachaça*-induced hangover and my chronic sinus infection. To top it off, the questionable-smelling guy next to me had commented all night on every single turbulence bump we hit. There is always turbulence traversing the equator in an airplane. Unseasoned travelers, and most people in general, don't interpret basic body language like reading or fake sleeping (even while wearing sleep blinders) as a sign of not wanting contact, contact meant to ease the personal angst wrought from the thought of hurling through the air in a heavy metal box at thirty-five thousand feet above terra firma.

After finally landing at the Los Angeles airport, I took my prayer back, God-blessing the USA as I always do when I step off the plane and onto home turf. Stumbling through the terminal like a zombie, I numbly followed the signs to immigration, baggage claim, and customs. The United States, and very few of its distant relatives from western Europe, have a highly organized travel infrastructure, requiring little energy, even less thought, and no stress for a traveler to get where they are headed. Most people with extensive international travel experience will tell you of this commonly held view of the United States. The polar opposite occurs when traveling in emerging markets. Confusion and stress reign once south of the 32nd degree parallel.

Perhaps the exception is Venezuela, where the locals have perfected the low-stress arrival. Arranging a "tourist service VIP pickup"—many things in Latin America are either VIP or "world famous,"— is code for arranging something on the sly or very expensive. Usually both. In Caracas, the service (usually a man wearing a entirely too dark and far too warm wool suit) picks you up from the jet way, slides you past immigration via an unmarked door as an unidentified third party grabs your bags and shakes hands happily with a wink and smile with the customs guards, and you are on your way, usually out another side door, and occasionally even the front door. The Venezuelan method is VIP but not quite "world famous" service. The arrival and departure experiences are not all positive. The Venezuelan departure adventure is as unpleasant as the arrival experience is pleasant, in both difficulty and stress level, not to mention personal safety. The stress begins as you leave isolated Caracas, which is located in a lush volcanic bowl of a valley, and travel from there down to the coastal airport in a circa 1970 U.S. sedan with questionable brakes, nonexistent steering, and bald tires. If you ever arrive for your departure otherwise, you are the president, or I don't believe you. The departure gives one an idea of the excitement and gut-wrenching stress that Columbus must have felt when setting sail for the New World.

Back in the comfortable confines of the United States I finally let my travel guard down: put my watch back on, move my car keys to my pants pocket, slip my passport into its hiding spot in the briefcase, and look for the appropriate sign so that I can shuffle out to the long-term parking shuttle pickup spot. And then the tiredness sets in. The resultant jet lag from flying west from Latin America (*yes west; look at your atlas*) wipes you out unexpectedly. The jet lag is not special, but rather garden variety, and it comes with the requisite headaches, restlessness, heavy eyeballs, and muscle fatigue. Probably mine is made worse by the frequency of the occurrence. After all, the jet lag experienced when going to Europe is always more severe—most people will tell you going east is far worse on the body than west. I think whether you are going out or heading home also plays a factor in the level of the lag. It is like a summer car trip when you are a kid. Getting there always is quick and easy, because you are excited for the adventure. The way back home takes twice as long and is almost unbearable. Anyway, a day or two of rest, good food, and beverages coupled with exercise for blood flow get me back to normal.

Nonetheless, the jet lag, the sheer physical toll put on you by international travel, can make you question why you've gotten yourself into this job in the first place. Why do it to yourself?

Typical Reasons to Be Involved in International Business

Most international business people do not necessarily get into the work by choice, but rather by accident or necessity. Why did you buy this book? Maybe you are a student—after all, I hope all international business students, or even graduate-level marketing students, find this to be compulsory reading someday. Most likely you are not a student, but you still find yourself turning these pages.

Companies growing into international markets typically do so as a reactionary measure to an opportunity that presents itself. The majority of fellow international business folks I have met were forced into the position in this type of manner. I hypothesize that that is one reason why many companies experience difficulty with getting international business started and experience a host of problems not only when they get started but especially as the business outside the United States grows. It is like an athlete not being properly trained, starting out with bad technique, and struggling over time to improve after those bad habits are an ingrained part of their game.

Those who choose international business as a profession, or those plunged into the fray of international responsibility for a business, have the daunting task to not only understand many of the fundamental issues pertinent to international business, but also to advocate and push for the constant education of those you work with in order to make the company adapt to the real issues you will face as you implement and grow your business.

Getting started in creating and implementing an international business is the most difficult part. There are a few categories of readers of this book. First are the students who are trying to learn everything they can for their future. I won't talk about this category here. The second category includes those whose companies have identified the need for international expansion, and you have been somehow anointed as the responsible party for the firm's decision. Congratulations—roll up your sleeves. The third, and most common, category includes those within a company who have a role in a functional area (e.g., marketing manager, sales director, business development manager, chief operating officer, chief marketing officer, chief sales officer, and others), who recognizes a reason to expand (usually opportunity or survival), and who realizes they don't know the first thing about going about expanding the business beyond the border.

Whether you are in the second or third category described above, the first thing you must do in the most professional way possible is to convince your managers and the company decision-makers that international opportunity exists. Even if a company has made some decision to enter international markets, in many organizations the need or opportunity for international business is not obvious. Another common challenge is gaining buy-in for a new corporate strategy in a long, or at least, political process that requires a certain amount of vetting, meetings, presentations, lunches, and the like in order to get the right people in the organization to get on board. I cannot tell you how to navigate the political waters in your firm, as you must do that yourself. I cannot suggest who needs to be on board, which functional areas in your particular firm are needed to allow smooth sailing, who approves investment, blesses marketing expenditures, okays sales plans, or dictates legal or administrative expenditures. You're on your own there. However, I can tell you the information you'll want to share. Read the rest of this book, and you'll be on your way.

Learning the Basics of International Business

There are textbooks on international trade and international marketing. There are excellent trade resources available from the United States, Canadian, and other governments. Some resources are highly recommended reading. Most texts are either functional (accounting, finance, marketing, operations, human resources) or socioeconomic–geopolitical (trade theory, globalization, fair trade, etc.), but they will not assist in practical applications to get you started or to convince management to spread its wings into the rest of the world.

There are no guidelines for the international business development professional. I work and live near Silicon Valley, the supposed center of the technology and business universe, and there is not one professional working group that fosters international market development. There is no guide to check out at the library that explains what you need to know in order to assess the international opportunity for your firm. There is no professional organization for the international market developer. Textbooks on the subject are few and far between, and they rarely are written by anyone with actual business experience.

> *Helpful Hint:* **Job security** for those who can get international development experience is real, and so the effort to undertake the talk is worth it by most measures. It is not uncommon for those in international business to be recruited regularly and not always because of domestic economic success. There is a reason these positions are so difficult to fill—the basic skills are acquired through experience rather than education or aptitude tests. There are a number of skills to develop to create your own international business portfolio that will allow you to make the right business decisions for your firm. Many of these skills, these tools, are discussed in the pages of this book.

People have told me many times that there are plenty of resources to learn about international market development. So why is it so difficult then? Perhaps the need for international market development as a discipline is not clear. After all, isn't that why we have such resources as the U.S. Department of Commerce, or local trade advocacy agencies, or even chambers of commerce? But these entities do not transact business, and their goals and mandates are quite dissimilar. They offer government programs and governmental (or quasi-governmental) resources for businesses. For actual business people, these resources will not assist you in developing the skills necessary to build international business. These agencies and their services, discussed more later in this book, are well-meaning and have their place as another resource used by the international market development individual, but they do not take the place of the skills required to build international business. The best simile I can give you is hitting a golf ball. You can read a book about striking a golf ball, and you can subscribe to a golf magazine, or even join a country club. But until you actually hit a golf ball and play golf, you really won't know how to handle yourself out on the course when trying to physically hit the ball off the first tee.

Think Global, Act Local

Increasing the difficulty in getting started, the world is comprised of thousands of distinct business and socioeconomic cultures. There are hundreds of countries in the world. Mexico is an apple, and Argentina is an orange, while Greece is a grape, the Dominican Republic is a watermelon … well, you get the picture. You cannot assume going in that a broad-brush approach mirroring your home-market business and marketing mix will solve your business challenge or provide you with the information to adequately assess all markets. The world is a basket of mixed fruit! Basing your international business strategy on regional issues is one thing, but implementing a blanket approach across multiple markets based on what you found to be successful in one country is a recipe for disaster. Ask Chevrolet about their "Nova" cars built for the Americas market in the 1970s.

The mantra of "think global, act local" is a true blue strategy for success in international business. Jack Welch's famous approach to embrace globalization is a rarity. At GE, he implemented a "localized" form of globalization that has proved successful throughout the years he has been at the helm. California's Monterey Institute of International Studies (where I teach occasionally at their Fisher School of Business MBA program) offers a regular curriculum in "globalization," or the need for a localized business approach for international business. Like this book, the approach is direct, simplified, and logical, and it allows students to glean the importance of modifying a marketing mix to international business.

When leading an international development effort, you are in essence taking a general philosophy and adapting it to whatever your business circumstance is. Rather than provide examples of this type of business effort ad nauseam, just keep in mind, as you read through this text, that in each case and with respect to each business issue, a strategic mind must be at work in taking larger business issues and applying a local spin to tailor the right solution for any given market. This approach will help your business efforts from at least two perspectives.

First, you will have formulated a general strategy to guide the manner in which you will approach markets. For example, suppose the issue you are considering is promotional marketing efforts for mass media campaigns to sell consumer auto parts, and you know from experience

6

in the United Kingdom and United States that the best medium for advertising is radio due to cost, demographic scope, and impact. If you are building your business strategy for South Africa, for example, you might assume that radio is similarly the best choice for marketing your auto parts to the masses. Once you actually evaluate the South African market, you need to ensure that a radio campaign will provide you with the best opportunity to achieve the same outcome for the same reasons as in the other markets (in this case, the United Kingdom and the United States). You may discover, however, that the audience differs, or that messages of this type (in this case, auto parts for sale) are not traditionally relayed through this medium (radio). Rather than make a losing effort to shove the message through the wrong channel, do some investigation to identify the best approach to delivering your message; in other words, in South Africa, what is the best media tool to use to distribute your message to the masses? As long as the same message is appropriate for the new market (note: the message used in one market may be wrong for the new market, but there may be another way to achieve the same results by varying the message or promotion in the market), you will have a better chance of success.

The second result of this tact is that you will more efficiently approach the majority of markets. That is, it is likely that your success in the primary markets is the result of a reasonable strategy and is based upon a specific need and correct approach to the business promotion. Therefore, if the product is the right fit for your move into new international markets, the ones that will prove a better fit for your product likely will be accepting of a similar message and similar method of getting it to market. We will spend a decent amount of time in chapter 3 understanding why it is so important to prioritize markets, and the subsequent implications from doing so.

Helpful Hint: **The downside of opportunism**. If you don't bother to properly plan and articulate a strategy, the costs of entering secondary- or tertiary-level priority markets can be both expensive and time consuming. Research and local market knowledge (however you tap into it on a case-by-case basis) will assist in ferreting out the costly markets so you can focus your attention elsewhere. Just remember that along with "think global, act local," it is also useful to avoid forcing Western practices into markets where it is (with some knowledge) not the best solution. Freeing yourself from your cultural perspective enough to appreciate and value the difference in markets around the world will allow you to accept, integrate, and properly evaluate markets from an international rather than domestically oriented perspective.

International market development is a new and unique expertise that requires incorporation of a firm's entire business model. It is challenging and can be quite enjoyable due to its international nature and its difference from business as usual in the home market. I hope you enjoy it—now on with the work.

2

Identifying Potential International Markets

It takes only a few moments in Switzerland to be overwhelmed with the sense you are in a hospital or a bank. The feeling is as strong as the sensation of always being near a campfire when in Brazil. The scent of smoke is in the air in Rio as it is in Sao Paulo and Manaus. Then there is Australia's likeness to California. Close your eyes standing on a street corner in downtown Sydney, and when you open your eyes you can easily be fooled into thinking you are in San Francisco. Mexico City's smog makes you feel like you are stuck in a dirty bottle. Paris has a unique museum quality. Belgium gives you the feeling a bull must have when in a China shop. Landing for the first time in Edmonton is like landing on the moon, and Germany's intimate family restaurants provide a sense of warmth and comfort, like being home.

Once you've had a chance to appreciate every land and culture for what it has to offer, you hit a condensation point at which you revert to the more basic underlying differences that allow you to qualify countries and the business culture atmospheres they present. For example, during the first few years I traveled to Chile, I appreciated the solemnity of the city of Santiago and attributed it to the social grace and conservative "European" culture. Years later, I know the charming yet cold culture is due to decades of severe government and Church-backed repression and a widespread nurtured fear of social activism. In other words, experience brings you back to basics.

The point is that regardless of what you think of Brazil being compared to a campfire, in all of its colorful glory, each market presents a unique environment. This uniqueness certainly extends to the business environment. Being able to identify and address these differences—that is, the ability to understand and make decisions based on market variables and how they impact your business—is a valuable skill. Some of the factors that are strikingly unique among various countries include the law, politics, and technology.

Legal Issues

Legal issues affect every aspect of international business. Domestically you don't really have to think about them because the environment is so structured to address any potential legal issue. When was the last time a marketing manager in the United States had to get legal counsel to approve a promotional campaign for a radio spot? Or when a retail buyer concerned herself with whether the importation certifications were correct for a toy doll on her store's shelves? The reason is because markets like the United States, with a long history of highly developed commerce and distribution systems, are so tightly controlled that burdensome international issues are non-issues at home. Keep in mind that the United States, United Kingdom, Germany, Japan, and other recognized leaders of open capitalist markets are not actually the world's most open and easiest places to conduct business.[1] Away from home it is a different ballgame.

You don't need a law degree to involve yourself in international development, but it sure would be helpful. Familiarity with trade law and contract law are most important. Basic development issues impacted by legal issues include trade law, importation regulations, channel distribution, contract law, product certification, intellectual property, product liability, and product and service warranties, among others. I'll touch more on these issues in the planning section (chapter 5) of this book.

Each step of the development process has a legal requirement that is bipolar. Not only does the organization have to consider protecting its intellectual property rights, but it also must ensure that it is not infringing upon intellectual property rights abroad. The developer's job typically is to manage the business aspects, but good knowledge of

---

1   Warren J. Keegan and Mark C. Green, 2005. *Global Marketing 4th Edition.* Pearson Prentice Hall, Upper Saddle River, New Jersey, pp.53.

the legal ramifications of your business activities will demonstrate your understanding of the total impact of your business endeavors to your management and counsel, again providing you more internal respect in the organization, more buy-in to your strategy, and ultimately commitment to the international effort.

For those of you saying to yourself, "I am not an attorney. What is this guy talking about?" Familiarity with the legal process and, particularly, the ability to identify which legal issues are important to consider in your business can be parlayed into easier understanding of local (international) law and how it impacts your business. Lack of this knowledge ultimately can lessen your control of the business and your standing in the organization. Perhaps most importantly, ignorance of these issues increases your organization's liability risk and decreases your likelihood of success in international markets.

To effectively manage international business, knowledge of relevant legal issues is extremely helpful. Whether you are responsible for bringing a new product or service to market for the first time or are simply adding to your product count, getting the product into the country, into stores, and into the homes of your customers involves many legal challenges and potential hang-ups that are best to understand and prepare for in your planning process. Know who your counsel is—not just the individual, but also the constraints under which you are working. Your counsel will tell you what is important if you bother to ask!

Helpful Hint: **Keep your legal counsel updated**. Your legal department is a cost center fought over by various groups, and typically their international focus is given some level (sometimes high, usually low) of priority in the business. Keeping counsel updated on your efforts to the extent they might affect them is wise. Warning them of potential future work is even smarter. Many attorneys have some interest in legal issues with a foreign basis. They all have an interest in protecting their company's business interests. Therefore, they are natural allies in your international development efforts. Involving your legal counsel to provide input into the decision-making process is even smarter still. They will be more likely to support your efforts if they are involved in the process.

In some cases you will have difficulty gaining internal legal support, which can be a huge barrier to your efforts. For example, if you know there will be legal issues to manage that are outside your scope, and you know that help is not going to be provided, you may need to alter your strategy or even your prioritization of certain markets. Any potential legal obstacles should be addressed in your planning process and included in your reports to senior management; you'll want to ensure that they understand the constraints under which you are working. As always, you can choose your battles for support internal to the organization, but choosing them wisely and with a mind to the strategic importance that today's issue represents can improve the response you receive from your legal and management groups going forward.

In other cases, an organization does not manage its legal resources well and may allow the international business developer to run roughshod over the legal process and create future legal problems for the organization. This is a too-common occurrence. Just because the intellectual property rights or importation regulations or product liabilities are not understood won't necessarily keep you from engaging in international commerce. But ignorance will not be a successful plea in court either!

U.S. companies are bound to the U.S. Foreign Trade Anti-Corrupt Practices Act as passed by Congress. This law binds all U.S. citizens to act ethically in international trade practices and holds us to the letter of the U.S. law while involved in foreign business transactions. Remember that other countries do not necessarily hold its citizens to such standards. European companies have the ability to account for what U.S. guidelines would consider corrupt practices as a line item on the income statement. To be fair, the OECD (Organization for Economic Co-Operation and Development) has tightened the rules against these types of practices in recent years, but still there is a culture of permissiveness for these activities in EU companies.[2] This fact, regardless of the moral dilemma it presents, means that in some cases your foreign competitors may be in a better competitive position, depending on the country market and customer you are dealing with in your business.

---

2   OECD. *Revised Recommendation of the Council on Combating Bribery in International Business Transactions*. Paris, France: OECD, 1997.

There are more than just risks of violating criminal code when engaging in international business. Firms are also beholden to the legal structure that dictates your international business activities. Contract law governs the business relationships typically entered into in international business. Legal requirements exist everywhere, and legal problems can be time consuming and costly to manage. Once a contract is signed, the organization will have responsibilities per the terms of the agreement. Twice I inherited situations where my predecessor had haphazardly signed rights away to certain markets. The result was a huge waste of resources in the time it took me to clean everything up—and senior management certainly saw the time and resource drain on other departments. Too much wasted effort supporting lame-duck international distributors is a recipe for disaster—not to mention the loss of goodwill likely to be experienced well into the future. This type of mismanagement is one of the things that cause domestic senior managers to be less than supportive of international development efforts.

Every organization's internal commitment to its international efforts changes over time. Good years and bad, new management, domestic pressures, trade policy changes, old guard versus new guard—all affect international focus in the organization. Networking within the organization, and continuous attention to maintaining—not burning— bridges, will help in the long term in securing the resources you require. You never know when the CFO with a domestic focus will retire and a new guard will arrive to support your interests. The legal issues in a previously untouchable market may become manageable with the changes, so be alert to them and act accordingly.

Typically, outside counsel may be necessary for a variety of corporate decisions, but the businessperson in charge has some responsibility to know what issues the business is faced with. Studying NAFTA telecommunications regulations has helped me understand the high-level impact the agreement has on our business. In many cases, however, I have sought out the input of international counsel or customs brokers for formal declarations regarding a specific business issue.

Trade Agreements and Taxation

Regional trade agreements may not only affect your direct business. For example, understanding Mercosur trade issues (encompassing four

Latin American countries: Argentina, Brazil, Paraguay, and Uruguay) for your business may change a strategic approach to your business in the southern cone countries. Also, free trade agreements (FTAs) between Mexico and Chile or negotiations between the European Union and South America may impact your business planning. Someone in the organization must be the scout for these issues, and such responsibility almost always rests with the international manager, who must be competent to evaluate the legal issues for the corporation.

More specifically for regional and country analyses, the basis for law varies country by country. Establishing a business partnership in Peru may require local (Peruvian) representation, while conducting business in Argentina might be entirely free of cumbersome legalities. The United States may have a competitive disadvantage to some European competition due to bribing practices, where in other markets U.S. competitiveness may be an easier fit. Tax issues may cause you to think twice about putting an office in Mexico City, while tax advantages make it more palatable in Caracas. Tax advantages may vary based on where a service or product is invoiced from. Companies should evaluate the consequences of invoicing from different country locations, as sometimes it is advantageous and other times it may happen to be disallowed in the country you are invoicing to, depending on the local structure your firm has in that market. An example of this situation is what happened to Cisco in Brazil in 2007.[3] Cisco Brazil executives were arrested for allegedly using "companies based in tax havens such as Panama, the Bahamas and the British Virgin Islands to avoid paying import taxes in Brazil. Officials accused Cisco of systematically understating the value (approximately $500 million) of merchandise it imported in order to pay less tax and of issuing falsified receipts." A cursory review of the typical legal issues surrounding your business (intellectual property, importation, local content laws, labor issues, taxation of foreign corporations) should be considered on a case-by-case basis. Also, if you have fiduciary responsibility for the corporations, who do you think goes to jail when something goes terribly wrong?[4]

---

3   "Cisco staff arrested in Brazil tax inquiry," Suzy Jagger, Times Online, www.timesonline.uk, October 18, 2007.

4   "IBM Execs Face Argentine Arrest," Reuters, June 2, 1998 (excerpt from www.wired.com).

Politics

Political structures surely are different in most countries. Where the democratic process is a long-held truism in the United States, Canada, and Europe, this is not the case for most of the rest of the world. Political issues directly impact all aspects of business. Protectionist practices stave off external investment with high trade tariffs to keep you out, while open economic markets offer lower barriers to entry. Even if a country is open to trade, there may be regional or state laws to protect national business interests. Tax law is implemented as a political as much as an economic tool. In Brazil, an import rate may be low, but regional manufacturers of goods may be entitled to breaks in sales or transaction taxes that importers of goods are subject to. Regional trade agreements between countries may also impact (positively and negatively) your ability to grow your business into neighboring markets.

For example, my business had a client, an e-commerce firm, who wanted some guidance regarding their invoicing practices. This firm managed their service provided from their U.S. headquarters, but ran a subsidiary operation in Brazil and had customers in Chile. Based on input from the client's Chilean agents, they were concerned that a withholding tax could be applied if they invoiced their Chilean clients from the United States, thus potentially reducing their received revenue from the Chilean client base. Once we analyzed the situation, we were able to determine that the nature of the services our client provides required withholding tax be applied to the invoiced amount whether invoiced from the United States or from Brazil. Additionally, since Chile is not part of the Mercosur free trade area (even though technically they do have special tax arrangements with the countries who comprise the Mercosur, including Brazil), if the company invoiced its Chilean clients from Brazil, then a local Brazilian tax structure would apply for the exportation of services. Given these circumstances, it became clear that our client should do their invoicing from the U.S. parent company and make some determinations regarding their ability to raise market pricing in order to compensate for the local Chilean withholding taxes. Understanding the political tax structure, then, requires knowledge of import and export regulations as well as the internal regional issues that might impact your organization's product or service.

Other politically controlled issues that are less obvious than tax code issues can make a difference to your business. Repatriation (or a government's legal but forced reacquisition of private entity's assets) is all too commonplace in emerging markets. Real estate policies may provide risk in Mexico to a major capital infrastructure investment, while in the EU or in Panama, laws provide more equal rights to nonresidents (again knowing the history of both countries tells much about any important government or social position). The Venezuelan government has a history of repatriating energy and telecommunications businesses. As Michael Porter, author of *Competitive Advantage of Nations,* argued early on in his career, the government policy of nations may support or hinder those natural advantages, which in turn affect business opportunity.[5] The international market developer has an advantage (or at least can mitigate identified risk) when he or she understands which issues are important and how they might impact his or her business.

Generally, the good news is that world governments are increasingly more open, and their markets are more competitive and open to foreign investment and financial participation. In fact, in some respects, especially with trade law and tariff agreements, the United States is lagging.

Technology

The world's technology infrastructure is beginning to even out with the implementation of Internet and mobile-based technologies. Although penetration levels vary widely, most markets with technological capabilities are implementing the same or similar technology worldwide. In those markets with rudimentary technological capabilities, things are different, and understanding this difference is important to developing your business strategy in a particular country. For example, with regard to telecommunications technology, the network infrastructure in Brazil rivals that of Belgium rather than Bangladesh. Telecommunications and data networks will impact how information is transferred and disseminated in a country, which in turn will impact your business, both strategically and directly. For example, in 1999, the state telecommunication company in Sao Paulo, Brazil,

---

5   Michael Porter. *Competitive Advantage of Nations.* New York: Free Press, 1990).

had a reported seven-million-person waiting list for a new phone line. If you were considering developing a business presence in this area, you would need to ask yourself the following questions: How fast are they installing new lines? What level of infrastructure is currently in place? What will it look like in one to five years? How will this affect any strategy or goals you might have already developed? How will these technology issues impact your business? How will technology advances in the markets where your firm currently conducts business be deployed in the markets you are considering to enter next? It could mean nothing and it could mean everything, and that is why you want to understand the technology.

The technological gains of developing markets are impressive and dynamic. Archaic technology systems are being updated with the world's very latest and greatest—typically at a hefty price to governments and large enterprise—in order to begin providing consumer benefits to their customers and citizens. Incorporating knowledge of the technology issues into your organization's strategy is a fundamental piece of the planning process and a possible key to the success of your enterprise. I'll spend more time on how technology impacts market development activities in chapter 12.

3
Traveling Safely

The swarm of soliciting taxi drivers just outside the terminal is bathed in ferocious street noise. Billowing plumes of exhaust emanate from most of the vehicles. Remember, Mexico's smell is exhaust. It was in 1994, and it is in 2009. On one of those rare occasions where I don't arrange a pickup from the hotel, I expect delays coupled with theater, and I am rarely disappointed.

I had long lost my cool before I launched out into the always-busy traffic in the back seat of a late model suburban. My anger was targeted at the taxi host (not the driver, but the guy who escorts you from the payment counter to where the vehicles are lined up outside the airport) who claimed that all VIP taxis had been spoken for, except for the one about five vehicles back with no way out (in Mexico City, a VIP taxi is usually more comfortable and somewhat nondescript, allowing for a supposedly comfortable if not safe ride into the city center). He provides the standard offer to let me ride in a compact yellow taxi that advertises the airport, and even more so the fact that the occupant is a tourist. I curtly decline and demand a driver. I explain I am not an idiot, that I have been here before, *and* I paid the extra twenty pesos for the big car (it's only two and half dollars, but it has nothing to do with relative amounts of money). Citing my *medio chilango*, or half Mexico City–Mexican, status does the trick, and he finally puts me in the suburban at the front of the line, and off we roar into the door-to-door traffic.

The process of getting into the can usually takes a good five to ten minutes, and you have to allow things to progress with periods of silence mixed with outbursts of emotion, but never *really* lose your cool—this is the case with any negotiating in Mexico, and in fact much of Latin America—or you won't go anywhere. Before the black, oversized truck pulls away from the curb, the taxi host tries his luck for a tip, at which I reply, "What have you given me but problems, Che?" The last barb "Che"—which refers to the Argentine reference to Che Guevara, the modern South American revolutionary who was a contemporary of the Castro brothers—is slang loosely equal to "dude" in California or "bradda," "bro," or "bra" in Hawaii, indicating a familiar endearment one uses to refer to friends. The reference "Che" makes the point that I know my way around Latin America, am insulted by the wait, and am using an Argentine phrase to close the conversation, leaving the guy with a bad taste in his mouth. No one in Latin America loves the Argentines as much as the Argentines. Hopefully he will remember and treat me better next time.

--

I was feeling untouchable in Mexico travel terms. It was March 17, and I'd been to Mexico a thousand times before (actually the real number is somewhere near one hundred, but "a thousand times" is a better translation of what I claim to the locals in Mexican Spanish). Nothing could surprise me in Mexico; I knew the people, their motivations, and their cultural sensitivities, and was riding a wave of current business success as a primary supplier of products to the second-largest company in Mexico.

After the morning meeting in the northwest of the city, I traveled southeast to the *Plaza Cuicuilo* to meet my customers for lunch and afternoon meetings. To the chagrin of my boss, I rarely schedule more than two meetings a day in Mexico City, as the commute is always worse than expected. Sometimes worse than that. Even though you may be left waiting in a reception area for hours on end, you should never return that Yankee slight to a Mexican. And when going across town, I always use private transportation due to the increase in street violence. Altercations with the bad element do not tend to improve your cultural affinity for any place. I've endured car accidents, taxi drivers brandishing a handgun, and other sordid encounters along the way.

Since it was St. Patrick's Day (the patron saint of my ancestral homeland and of my confirmation name), I was upset that I was not at home enjoying a game of cribbage with Dad, and drinking beer with the brothers, as Mom prepared the corned beef with cabbage. To forget my worries, I enticed my work friends (all locals) out to search for green beer. Mexico City, I soon discovered, does not serve green beer on St. Paddy's Day. After our third stop, a big dinner, lots of jokes, and squeezing the life out of the city, we called it a night. Departing from the Zona Rosa, we headed toward the Angel of Independence to get me back to my hotel. Pedro was driving, and the streets were empty, save the famous sewer rats that remained cloaked in darkness. It was after getting halfway around the traffic circle that the flashing lights came out of what seemed every direction and bathed the car in red flashes. A quick flash to my watch revealed it was 3:00 a.m.

Screeching to a halt in dramatic fashion, the motorcycle cops parked one of the bikes against my door on the passenger side, I suppose blocking the escape path. The other cop had parked somewhere behind the vehicle. As if a gringo in a suit and Italian shoes would go sprinting away from them. *Great,* I thought.

I said to my friend, "What is going on, what did we do?"

"Nothing; just don't say anything and I'll take care of it."

"Whatever. Just get us the hell out of here. This is not a good scene."

Mexico City cops are notoriously corrupt and violent, and perhaps a bit legendary, especially after the dismantling of the once-feared *Federales,* who terrorized locals and tourists alike in the Mexican countryside. I suppose some group had to step in to take the infamy in such a dramatic society.

More drama. The cop edged his way slowly to the driver window, leaving his partner at the back right of the car. He walked loudly, and the soles of his over-weighted riding boots scraped the asphalt. At the window, he skipped pleasantries, positioning himself with his face behind his clipboard and his right hand relaxing clearly on the scratched and dimly worn butt of his service revolver, not a foot from my buddy's face.

"You made a serious traffic infraction on the circle, and we must take you into incarceration for six days. Have you been drinking?"

Six days? I wondered. *Did we run over a street vendor back there?* My smart-ass thoughts quickly vanished.

"Officer, good evening, what exactly was the infraction? Officer, I only had two beers with dinner about five hours ago."

"You've been drinking and made a serious traffic infraction. Get out of the car because we are taking you in."

"Officer, where will you be taking us and for what infraction?" The overuse of politeness and respect for authority, especially in a situation where one person maintains power, age, or both as in this case, can be over the top.

"A serious infraction, and I cannot disclose the location. Get out of the car."

Oh, shit, you've got to be kidding me. Bad apple. My mind was racing, and I looked down the street to check for witnesses, passersby, anyone who might improve the situation. Nobody was around. The city sat silent and dark. This was not St. Paddy's Day in Boston. I noticed we were parked in the shade of the trees lining the large avenue called the *Reforma*, which from any angle was hidden from most of the boulevard. A bad dream.

"Officer, can we pay our fine for the ticket in place of the jail time?"

The fat man shuffled to the back of the car to discuss bribes with his partner. I asked my buddy where they'd take us. He responded with no idea, and suggested it might be trouble. *Jesus, Mary, and Joseph. How do we get out of this?*

Back at the window, the man demanded six thousand five hundred pesos—about $700.

"Officer, I only have fifty pesos." My buddy was dry.

"Get out of the car."

"Wait! I have a hundred dollars." I always, without exception, carry a couple of hundred dollars on me, just for emergencies, and this seemed to fit the bill.

The officers regrouped and came back to call my bluff. I ended up paying him $200 in cash. He "didn't want my change, and get the hell out of here." I hadn't known that corrupt officials looked down on small bills.

Outwardly I'd remained calm, but I noticed my hands shaking a bit, and told my friend to get me to my hotel. He missed the exit once and barely got within a block on the next go around. He was rattled. The third try he dropped me off and suggested we keep what happened between him and me—more than anything I think because Mexicans like to think Mexico is nicer than it really is. I don't think it's more complicated than that.

If I'd had an option to fly home that evening, it may have been the last night of my international business career. It took a couple of beers and a lot of swearing, coupled with country damnation, to get me to sleep that night. The next morning, stepping through the brown air as I exited the hotel, I acknowledged my reality—knowing that "bad" is everywhere, and you just have to try to avoid it. I decided to keep my job, and I swore off early-morning travel in the great city of Mexico.

Know What You Are Getting Into

An acquaintance of mine who is involved in international trade policy issues within organizations related to the CalChamber (the California Chamber of Commerce) in Sacramento once told me a few great stories of his international work in developing and managing Fairchild Semiconductor's international business in the 1960s. The tail end of his career involved international market development work with his own firm in the 1970s. He had traveled to Brazil during the various military dictatorships and had flown in and out of China, Japan, and Hong Kong on various occasions. He helped several U.S. companies begin their business in Japan. As my friend had been a trailblazer in international market development, I asked him if he ever sat down and wrote anything about his business experiences. He told me he didn't want to write a travel book—way too many of those around. I hope that some day Jerry will read this book and then write a book of his own about the adventures he experienced and the markets he opened to U.S. business. Meanwhile, I'll tell you what you should know about international traveling before you get in over your head.

Depending on how old you are and your station in life, you may find international travel an adventure or a burden. Regardless of how old you are, a mother, a girlfriend, a spouse, or children will be worried and will expect regular phone calls while you are overseas. If you are fortunate to have a supportive group of family and friends, your international travel can provide the experiences of a lifetime. Anytime you can enjoy the moment while on the road in pursuit of creating a successful business experience, it can truly double the satisfaction of the experience. You will meet new people, learn new cultures, learn of the world's history firsthand, and gain more knowledge of your own place in the world by knowing more about what lies beyond your borders.

While traveling, there are a few tips that can help keep it a safe experience. Knowing how to stay safe while traveling, especially in this time of war around the world, is not only important for your personal safety but also for the durability of your career and your firm's interests internationally. One bad experience can change the outlook on you or your firm's prospects internationally, allowing the risk of personal danger to heavily weigh against any opportunity for business growth or profitability.

Knowing something about the country you travel to can automatically provide a safer experience, simply because you will know what to expect. It is easy to find information regarding the hospitality of any given market and its general state of safety. The U.S. Department of

State is a prime example of a good source for information.[6] Other government sources, such as local embassies and commercial offices, will advise you regarding the current state of safety and travel recommendations via fax, telephone, or e-mail. These types of advice are especially helpful when you travel to politically unstable (for example, Colombia) or economically unstable (example, Russia) markets where crime rates may be higher given the current socioeconomic environment. A variety of Internet-based travel information portals[7] also provide updated travel safety information. Checking these resources is typically a prudent part of the planning process discussed earlier in this book, and safety should be weighed accordingly.

In the late 1990s, when I was traveling frequently to Latin America, I completely avoided traveling to Colombia due to the high rate of kidnapping and murder. I simply considered the risks to my personal safety during my planning process, and my upper management never had a problem with my reasoning. Obviously, there is a correlation between civic unrest and personal safety, and civic unrest usually affects economic stability levels in a given market. In other words, if your personal safety is at risk, then doing business in that market is probably a high-risk venture.

A positive by-product of this extensive travel was an ability to manage a significant budget and spend money in a strategic manner. So even though the ability to build a beachhead was far down the line, the ability to manage a budget strategically (with the idea being that I had to at least get the business analyzed and planned over a twelve-month period, including a specific budget number managed to), prepared future efforts to manage a budget based on a beachhead and prioritization-of-markets strategy.

Fast forward to 2008, and much of Africa is still in political, civil, and economic turmoil. I am a cofounder of a business in Johannesburg, South Africa. South Africa is one of the safest countries in sub-Saharan Africa and is the economic powerhouse of the continent. Regardless, due to the ongoing strife and political unrest in the region and the lousy

---

6   U.S. Department of State travel information and warnings can be found at http://travel.state.gov/travel.

7   Two good information portals include http://www.safetraveler.com and http://www.fco.gov.uk.

treatment of (mostly black African) foreigners, I have no current plans to visit our local operation. I do plan to visit in the future, most likely when the Soccer World Cup event is held in 2010; but most likely my visit to our offices will be brief. In addition, my business partners who do plan on visiting in early 2009 plan to utilize Cape Town (the resort city to the far southwestern coastline of the country) as their base, and I will be surprised if they actually venture inland to "J-Berg" to visit the headquarters of the company in which they own a large stake.

Utilizing a philosophy of smart and safe traveling will allow you more likelihood of enjoying your travel and making the most of your international business.

Helpful Hint: **Business travel insurance**. Beyond looking out for yourself, your organization hopefully will care about the safety and well-being of its employees, namely you. A safeguard the organization can utilize is travel insurance. Some insurance carriers will provide employer insurance for its employees who travel internationally, with emergency situation insurance should you get in a real pickle or become a victim of crime. When I was working for a firm in the late 1990s, they carried a travel policy on me that would medevac me to the United States in the event I became severely injured and would pay for emergency assistance should I ever be kidnapped, or worse. Luckily it never had to be used, but it was somewhat reassuring to know that my family had some insurance on my well-being. I never was overly worried about my own safety, since I traveled only to the places I chose.

4

Cultural Considerations in International Development

We'd already spent several thousand dollars in local legal fees on the acquisition of an Internet service provider (ISP). My business partners and I also had an incoming investment pending from a publicly traded company. That deal was awaiting the ISP acquisition to close in order to confirm the investment in our new Argentine venture.

I picked up the phone, as I had every other day over the past four months, to ask our local Argentine partner when the contract would (finally) be inked. "Any day now; the seller has requested just a few small changes in the contract, and with that we should confirm everything." I had the same conversation at least ten times over three months; the seller dragging his feet without rhyme or reason. I got off the phone and called American Airlines to book another trip to Buenos Aires. A week later, the final negotiation session discussion went something like this:

Me: "Fausto [seller], the attorneys have vetted the contract and there is no future risk. Let's move this forward into due diligence by signing a letter of intent and then the contract within two weeks."

Fausto: "I have one small request. The payment for the shares. We have agreed the buyers would secure the final payment in escrow. I would only now ask that you pay interest to me [Argentine rates, currently above 25 percent] for that period the payment is in escrow. Interest on the entire acquisition price."

He must be kidding, I thought; but of course he wasn't.

Since our local partner had prepared me for this tactic prior to the negotiation, one of our partners had equipped me with a brilliant response. So, my response to Fausto was this: "Interest is important to us as well. What say you that we pay you all of the payments upon signature of the contract, and you discount the same value in interest against the payment?"

Silence.

And so it had gone for months.

Cultural Differences and Their Impact on Business

Several years into it I had come to realize that generations of political and economic oppression have created a culture of risk-averseness and abhorrence to individual decision making in Argentine business. On the face of it, this is a strong statement, but one based in my individual understanding of Argentine culture.

Cultural understanding is a slippery slope, so you should self-monitor to ensure that you articulate cultural business issues only as they relate to your business activities. An example is that if you are in your first formal meeting with a local partner, client, or vendor, do not mention a random issue of relative cultural importance, particularly one that might be negative. In Argentina, for instance, you wouldn't bring up the train wreck that is the current federal government. In Chile, you wouldn't try to understand how the public tolerated decades of totalitarian oppression. In Venezuela, you wouldn't nonchalantly bring up U.S. political opposition to President Chavez. In South Africa, you wouldn't talk about apartheid. Once a rapport is established, and perhaps in a more appropriate setting (over lunch, dinner, coffee, drinks, and outside of the office), you might have a genuine interest in and be looking for a valuable opinion on some cultural issue, and only then, in a "social" setting, would it be appropriate to ask. It also may serve to strengthen your personal tie with your contact. However, touchy cultural issues are something that you shouldn't dive into if you don't know what you are talking about, don't know where the line to stop is, and especially if you do not have a decent sense for the reaction or personal view of the person you are talking with. Otherwise, you may end up defending statements that may seem arbitrary or ignorant. In this case, your contact is less likely to have confidence in you, and therefore your ability to engage in business with him or her is reduced (whether or not they articulate that to you).

Decision makers in a market-based, entrepreneurial society (i.e., the United States, Singapore, or most of the EU) are those who have demonstrated leadership and management acumen to vault them to the task. In much of Latin America, the wealthy, educated class holds most all of the management positions, and therefore there is not the same level of training and skill set as an American might expect. What results is decision by committee, and even worse, ultraslow decision making that is so over vetted that many times the decision becomes moot by the time the decision maker has actually pulled the trigger.

To add insult to injury, a deal may be verbally confirmed for a long period of time without actual consummation of the agreement. This cultural proclivity begets inefficiencies throughout businesses, and it is not only because it is a time-honored tradition that the economy observes; in fact, it is a rule of the game.

Lesson in Cultural Differences

Textbooks on various cultures usually focus on the anthropological and social aspects of culture rather than on how culture impacts business. The history, language, and experiences of a people are certainly important. Social culture is the self-definition of any society. Therefore, if you expect to function effectively in a particular culture, you should develop an understanding of it and look through the cultural lenses of that culture when developing a business in international markets.

The basis for understanding cultural differences on a macro level is the understanding that social constructs are at the root of all cultures. For example, there is the contextual significance of cultural variables. Cultures are separated between high context and low context on a contextual field. One of the fundamental theories I use in my teaching[8]

---

8   Edward T. Hall. *Beyond Culture.* Anchor Books, New York, 1976.

explains this quite well. High-context cultures, those where interactions and meaning is important, value personal relationships, place import on aesthetics, and have a deeper requirement for trust, feeling, and personal knowledge. They also tend to need only a small amount of personal space and are accustomed to a larger degree of physical touching. Low-context cultures, by contrast, limit the importance of personal trust. Personal interaction is less important, relationships are not as personal, more personal space is required, touching occurs less, aesthetics are not as important, trust is not based on personal relationships, and feelings and personal knowledge are minimally important.

Places with high contextual cultures are Italy, Argentina, Mexico, Central America, much of China, and parts of Africa and Southeast Asia. I've touched on the personal knowledge required to buy a company in Argentina. In Nicaragua and much of Central America, if you are my friend, then your friend is my friend, and I would prejudge your friend as I have judged you. In Italy, as in much of Latin America, friends greet with a hug and many times a kiss (man or woman—it doesn't matter). In China, the color red is famous for signifying good luck, as is the number eight, and to a lesser degree, the number three. In other high-context cultures, it is common to expect little personal space and to rely a great deal on not only your business acumen but also your ability to foster and nurture relationships to thrive in business. Friends kiss when greeting and hug when departing, and creating a substantial business relationship can often take months to establish to the point where sufficient personal knowledge and trust is in place to transact business.

Another component to personal space is the importance of personal proximity or personal knowledge of those one communicates with. In high-context cultures, it is not only important to know personally those you do business—it is required. Personal communication is completely different in high-context cultures than in low-context cultures. Electronic mail, regardless of its importance in the United States, Canada, or northern Europe, is an afterthought in most high-context cultures. E-mail is not the preferred way to meet someone, and it is certainly not interactive enough to conduct business over. Interestingly, text messaging is wildly popular in high-context cultural markets. My theory is that instant messaging ("IM") protocols somehow satisfy the interactive nature of the communication, and so although it is not truly personal, it is still accepted. Generally in these markets the more personal the communication the better.

In-person meetings are the best way to get off on the right foot and to begin to create a relationship that can be utilized to build a business relationship—even if you have to travel a day to some remote locale. If your business opportunity justifies it, the recommended approach is to meet your contact in person. Follow-up via conference call is an acceptable option, but further visits in person provide intrinsically valuable cultural ties that not only lead to more vetted relations but more business. Not too long ago I was on a trip and was able to make personal contact with someone who later became an important and reliable contact for me in my business. The initial in-person meeting we had and the firsthand knowledge that was gained during that meeting provided that business contact with the comfort level needed to recommend me and our firm as someone to deal with, and it eventually positioned us better for the business.

Low-context cultures include parts of Asia (Singapore), North Central Europe (Denmark, Germany, the Netherlands), Scandinavia, the United States, and Canada (though the latter two are changing because of their high percentages of immigrants who are slowly by surely impacting the culture). In the United States, you might buy a car sight unseen off of Craigslist. In Germany, you might conduct a large business deal with someone over the phone without meeting face-to-face. In Scandinavia, friendships are based on personal knowledge and are not assumed. In many of these countries, aesthetics (the way something is presented or perceived or appreciated because of its color and physical attributes) are not as important as the material facts being presented. The opposite of high-context cultures, in low-context markets personal space is expected, and personal relationships are not important to transact business.

Helpful Hint: **The difference between high-context and low-context cultures**. As discussed above, understanding this difference is almost as important as knowing in which type of culture you are conducting business. Appreciating the implications of such issues as personal relationships can make or break your international development effort.

Communication Techniques

Language, verbal and physical, is the basis for communication. I agree with the experts who say that body language is significantly more important than verbal communications. This is not a book about verbal communication, and I assume that you have that part mastered, or at least understand your own strengths and weaknesses when it comes to the linguistics of another culture. There is a good amount of jingoism relative to dialectic patriotism in many parts of the world, notably so in Latin America. Just because you can order a taco on the street in Tijuana does not mean you can converse in familiar, collegial tones in Santiago de Chile. You must home in on language differences everywhere where the culture differs.

Sure, the languages spoken in Mexico and Chile are both Spanish, but they are as different from each other as they are from the Castilian of Argentina, the Castilian of Spain, or the Caribbean-influenced Venezuelan. If you speak like a Venezuelan in Argentina, they will treat you like one, rather than one of their own. You are how you communicate. In Argentina, there happens to be some camaraderie between Venezuela and Argentina, but if you typically speak Mexican Spanish in Argentina, I would recommend speaking American English instead. At least, then, you would be looked upon as someone from an economic power (assuming you don't push any notion of American dominance and annoy someone) rather than as someone from an equal-to-inferior economy trying to horn in on what is their part of Latin America. If you apply this same rule to virtually any country when considering the perception of language roots and dialects, you may gain a foothold in the countries you are trying to make business.

Of course, there is more to understanding a culture than knowing how to communicate and what the low-context and high-context implications of your business strategy will be given the markets you plan to do business in. Political and social history as well as social constructs are perhaps not as germane to business, but familiarity with these can go a long way when trying to understand why business is conducted in a certain fashion in one country and not in the neighboring one. For example, the history of the colonization and independence of a market can give you a perspective for a country's age, its systems of government, and its economic realities. The history of political advances since independence in many countries will provide a different level of knowledge. Recent history may shed light on policies that impact your company's business. Social history, although a bit more sensitive in many developing markets in the world, can tell you a lot about the people and how they behave in social and business situations. Also, understanding the social background of the market may give you a better sense of the underlying market demographics your company is dealing with there.

Cultural Identity

One of the impacts of cultural identity is that it tends to define a country. It defines how companies, individuals, and governments interact to make their world go around. Culture is what makes countries unique. The residents of a particular country share a combined set of historical and social experiences that create a paradigm of accepted behavior for all within their context. It is why earlier in the book I mentioned that e-mail is not the communication method of choice in much of the developing world. Then there is a U.S. concept called political correctness. Political correctness is communicating in a way as to consciously not offend another person, group, government, entity, etc., based on the social fabric or mores of their society. This concept doesn't specifically exist in most emerging economies, or many other cultures period. Examples of "being PC" in the United States are numerous. Two examples: one should not refer to a flight attendant as a stewardess, and one should not refer to a Native American as an Indian. In the former example, it is reasoned that a flight attendant is more than a waiter or waitress, and in the latter example it is reasoned that the geographic place name of India is not representative of the ethnicity of those being labeled. Such distinctions are quite American PC concepts. In the case of the word Indians, it is an identifier quite often used around the world, meaning "ethnically local," rather than any disparagement in associating native populations with the country of India, which is perfectly great in its own right (and not a disparagement).

In countries outside the United States, cultural sensitivity is still important, perhaps even more so; there typically is a well-accepted set of cultural fundamentals that define how one should act in society. In high-context cultures, the value of personal relationships and mutual respect is a very critical component of how society functions. When I fired a general manager at a company I owned in Argentina, I didn't tell him on the phone, and I certainly didn't send an e-mail (he might never have responded!). The termination act required a certain level of personal involvement in order to portray the gravity of the decision and the personal respect for the person being fired. Had I informed him any other way than in person, the impersonal method of firing him would have been interpreted as showing much disrespect toward him. I would have carried that with *me* from job to job, and company to company. So I flew the fourteen hours to Buenos Aires, found a few other things to do while I was halfway across the world, invited him to an after-work drink, and fired him. It was quite well accepted from a cultural standpoint.

Months earlier, I had called up my general manager in Argentina and asked him to make sure the next salesperson he hired was an intelligent, communicative, energetic, and beautiful young woman— preferably with long legs and who looked good in a skirt. I was just kidding about the legs and the skirt. Of course, I would get sued in the United States for making such a statement let alone a management directive. But Buenos Aires is not Seattle; nor is it Athens. In Seattle, political-correctness is religion. In Athens, you might not prefer a young woman as the face of your company. In many Latin American cultures, however, men are very receptive to the presence of a woman, and I would argue that they therefore make ideal salespeople, managers, and office receptionists. Women have been making significant professional advances in Latin America for many years now.

Until recently, you could smoke openly in Mexico City restaurants. Now it is more common to find separate spaces for smoking patrons. Even so, I would not hesitate to pull out a cigar and smoke it at the table, nor do I hesitate to open the door for a lady. In Canada, do either, and they will hang you from the nearest tree. The point, obviously, is to know what to do where and vice versa. Fitting into the landscape is important around the world. Knowing how to behave in the country in which you are doing business is necessary to get anything even started. In Seattle, I guess that chauvinistic tendencies are frowned upon, as would be lighting up a cigar at a restaurant. At the same time, someone who makes cultural judgments based on their home market (i.e., being politically correct when it is not required or desired) and who sneers at the same activities in a culture where those activities are accepted and expected probably won't be very successful doing business there in the long run.

5
The Importance of Strategy and Planning

I was surprised and dejected when I learned I had been downgraded to a cubicle from the comfortable office I'd enjoyed in my previous job. Of course the promotion in responsibility and the pay grade increase made the cubicle more bearable. I quickly realized, however, that the time on the road would make secured office space despised and wasted back home. I did have a nice networked computer, and so I dove right in to evaluating the inheritance my predecessor left behind. I had sales reports, a stack of manila, hanging folders with company information, a distributor training history, and a contact phone list. Turns out I would have been better off had I been left nothing at all and ignored the details my predecessor left behind.

A couple of days of analysis really put the financial performance of the business into perspective. Once the financial history (sales, training and demo investment, etc.) was triangulated properly to determine which distributor had a greater payback than their neighbor, it was plain that none of the distributor scenarios were positive. In fact, they all were losing propositions, and when I finally compared my analysis to the predetermined (i.e., I had no input) forecast and budget scenarios for next year, I thought to myself that making the business a success was nearly impossible. The problem (to be played out) was that the forecast was not reasonable, given thorough analysis of each market, the analysis which showed little distributor investment in money and time; a lack of ongoing training in a rapidly changing technology product segment; and the lack of market talent to build the business. Fortunately, my travel and expense budget was fairly substantial, so my cost structure would not make the expected results even more lopsided than anticipated.

As the first couple of weeks passed, I started to present these findings to my management team and started to set expectations that the financial expectations heretofore presented included assumptions that were yet to be confirmed from my perspective. Management, of course, didn't give a rat's ass about the incongruence of their forecasts versus historical revenue and margin numbers, but rather sent me off with marching orders that basically dictated that I figure out a way to make the numbers come to fruition. A publicly held company that regularly set out stock market expectations well in advance wasn't in the cozy position to change revenue and margin numbers on a dime. So therein was the challenge. It ultimately turned out to be a valuable exercise as far as career growth, because I had to totally dismantle then reestablish our firm's emerging market business.

Assessing Inherited International Business

Going about the evaluation of your current business can be a task that ranges in difficulty from not easy, to taxing, time-consuming, and "pull-out-your-hair" difficult. Even though you need to understand the hand you are dealt to begin, keep in mind that the evaluation and assessment of your firm's activities will most likely be an ongoing one. In case you are wondering when and how often you should be evaluating or reevaluating your international business—at least once a year, and certainly any time you are either starting out, considering placement of a beachhead operation, or evaluating a local presence. Each of these scenarios should instigate an evaluation of the international effort.

One of the key outputs of a successful assessment during your initial evaluation is to memorialize the evaluation information for the creation of your business plan. Using past and present information allows you to demonstrate a road map of how the company has fared based on a previous strategy, the company's current status in the international market, and how you plan for the company to reach its new goals considering your starting point. The ability to assess current activity and align it with planning goals is your first tactical step to building momentum toward management approval of your international planning efforts.

> *Helpful Hint*: **Categorize inherited information**. As a future planning exercise, categorizing and organizing your information will make it useful for the planning process, and ultimately, decision making. If you are just starting fresh in your firm's international effort, an evaluation step typically is not required, as you won't have any decent information to compare against your future targets. To assess the business you've inherited in a manner most easily articulated to other staff or management, create a basic SWOT analysis built around the marketing and financial performance of your company's international business. A SWOT (Strengths, Weaknesses, Opportunities, and Threats) is a utility planning tool since you can tailor it to what is relative and important in the way your firm manages and measures its business activities.

Metrics

Metrics, for the sake of this book, are the measures your company uses to gauge performance. Many times they are numbers like revenue, gross margin, net margin, return on investment, inventory turnover, operational measures, Web-site traffic, bandwidth usage, transaction analytics, and so on. More recently, metrics have come to include concepts only possibly related to numbers. An example is the notion of the "triple bottom line," which is a new, hot, buzz phrase in business schools. The triple bottom line is the company results relative to planet, people, and profit. Is the firm green and environmentally responsible? Are the firm's employees, customers, and vendors treated, trained, rewarded, and challenged in a way that satisfies individual and group stakeholders? Is the firm making money?

The following is a cautionary tale for those of you managing in a world of triple bottom line versus bottom line. After cofounding a small Web 2.0 company in 2005, I attended a Web 2.0 conference in San Francisco that was a highly regarded "meet-up" that allowed participants to select seminars to attend during a daily schedule. The couple of hundred attendees were mostly founders of other Web 2.0 start-ups in the Bay Area. Reading the agenda, I noted several breakouts that were of interest—community building, marketing, fund-raising, design, and the like. The breakout I most wanted to join was the "monetizing Web 2.0" breakout. I was one of only a small handful of attendees in this breakout. Maybe that is why so many Web 2.0 companies have never been able to make any money—because many of the businesses did not use any financial metrics.

"Financials" in traditional corporate terminology refer to the profit and loss (income) statement, the balance sheet (assets and liabilities), and the cash flow of the business. From an operational standpoint, financials are more personal in nature—that is, whatever numbers and measures are important to measuring the performance of your international activities. For example, financials for a firm's international market developer may include revenue and margin numbers, both relative to the business as a whole and broken down by country or market region. Revenue is the easy one to identify. Margin analysis tends to more difficult. Even seasoned managers have trouble with margin analysis. When considering margin analyses, developers should concentrate their margin analysis on the "contribution margin" of their business. Contribution margin is the amount of money remaining (i.e., the margin) that goes into the firm to pay for overhead of the business after all attributable variable costs associated with getting your product commercialized to the market are deducted.

Don't underestimate the work involved in evaluating margins when you are getting started. Margins are important. Margins influence, and may dictate, pricing strategies, which we'll get into in more detail later in this chapter. To fully asses your international businesses, you may need to break down the analysis such that you can truly treat each revenue-producing area of business as a business unit and then allocate the resources used to maintain each part of the business to come up with a true summary scenario for each market. For example, if you have a distributor partnership established in Mexico, there likely are some specific pieces of information you will want to look at. How much did it cost to get the distribution agreement set up? What were the training costs for the company? The travel costs required establishing the business relationship? The product development costs of getting products ready for entry in Mexico? What were the purchase terms and how did that impact margins? The cost to ship product to market? The taxes? The local support costs? The cooperative marketing costs? Advertising. Commissions. Personnel costs. Marketing. Trade shows. Samples. Development. And on and on.

Remember, when you are determining margins, you want to include the costs relative to *your* company, not anyone else's. If your predecessor was fortunate enough to get the distributor owner to travel to your home office for multiple trips for negotiations (this is highly unlikely!), then the actual cost of travel might be lower than if your firm bore the burden. It is important to include such information in your assumptions so that you can assess the opportunity cost associated with the business. A note of caution—the costs related to the existing business may or may not be the same related to your business going forward! You will have to be diligent in considering your entire business model to fully identify and understand the total actual costs associated with each market experience. Conduct a product-by-product contribution margin analysis and perhaps even a return-on-investment (ROI) analysis to conduct market-to-market (apples to apples) comparisons. So conduct one margin and financial analysis for the current business, but don't assume the results will absolutely be relevant to your future planning requirements.

Importance of Market Knowledge

Once your financial picture is as clear as it is going to get, you'll need to get familiar with your markets. In some cases, the business history will have been so bad and the return negative that you may opt to pass on traveling to that market, even if you have a distribution relationship to cancel in the near future. If the business was that bad, don't bother throwing good money after bad. The fact that you are aware of this and follow prudent evaluation steps usually will not be lost on management.

In the mid-1990s I inherited (twice, in two different businesses) distributors in Colombia that netted negative payback in both cases. Although for both companies I traveled extensively in the region (probably ten to fifteen trips annually to South America), including many multiple-stop trips, I never set foot in Colombia. I should also say that at the time, Colombia was one of the last places on Earth anyone would want to travel to, but that was secondary in my decision never to stop for business in Bogota.

There have been many times I have enjoyed a day or two prior to business meetings in an international market. One time I spent a weekend with an old classmate in Sao Paulo before meetings in Brazil. Many times I spent weekends in Paris meeting old family friends and touring favorite locales. I spent a weekend in Antwerp; another on a train in northern Spain; and many others on jaunts to the beaches and mountains of Mexico, Venezuela, and Peru. I even spent a weekend exploring some of the nearby jungle in Panama. All of these times I not only strengthened my cultural knowledge of the country I was in, but, more importantly, I also learned something new and fresh, something that couldn't be picked up from the front page of the newspaper or the Internet.

When Monday morning arrived, wherever I was, I had stories to tell, relating to them on their terms, in their culture, and with some local understanding. Invariably, the reaction to this was positive and forged a bond between me and those with home I interacted on a business basis. What is important to remember is that I didn't just spend free time in these places to help by business, particularly. I did it to learn more and to gain more local knowledge (while enjoying myself immensely) that I knew would allow me to increase my effectiveness as a businessperson in that country. And it always has helped, especially in Latin America, where their high-context cultures require a certain level of trust to interact at a significant level in business. That trust is based not only on the person your business associates know but the person they know about. It's like your parents might have told you when you were a kid—"you are your friends."

Helpful Hint: **Travel the region**. Traveling the region is critical to your success. It is quite difficult to have full knowledge of a market's potential or applicability to your business if you do not know it firsthand. Sometimes, logically, you won't have the luxury to travel the world in order to know if your widget is perfect for one market more than another based on your firsthand knowledge. Luckily for you the ability to research, communicate, and develop business today is much easier than when I started in 1994! You can learn a lot through the Internet (wikipedia.com and other sources mentioned previously); but the best way to utilize your own set of values and judgments is to base your decisions on your own experiences.

If you know your company will consider developing business in Mexico and Canada, you should travel those markets. If your business historically has been strong in Central America, then you probably want to see it firsthand. You might be surprised how much you can learn about your business on a couple of trips to a given country. I'd recommend focusing on seeing and knowing the cities that fit the typical profile for the business you are in. That is, if your product sells in rural areas, then avoid Mexico City, as it may not give you a read on the Mexican market as it applies to your business. If your business distributes to only value-added resellers (VARs) in major metro markets, then you should know Mexico City, Guadalajara, and Monterrey in Mexico, and Vancouver and Toronto in Canada, for example. A surprisingly little amount of money can be spent to learn a lot of valuable information for your organization.

In 2008 I attended a luncheon in Sacramento where the U.S. Assistant Secretary of State for the Western Hemisphere spoke about the Colombia–U.S. FTA, for which the approval process has been stalled in the U.S. Congress for political reasons. While at the event, I spent time to introduce myself to some of the others in attendance, as I normally do. One of the more memorable attendees was a California legislative trade analyst who surprised me mightily when she began quizzing me on the current nature of economic or business climates in South America. Even though she is a trade analyst and should have a macro understanding of what is going on internationally, I asked her why she was so in tune with such issues. She went on to surprise me by telling me how she'd recently been to the backwaters of Ecuador to fully evaluate the implementation of an energy project before weighing in on it as part of her course of business. She said the governor had mentioned to her and other staff that with respect to international trade, "You have to go to *know*." I give both she and Governor Arnold Schwarzenegger all the credit in the world. Words could not be truer.

Helpful Hint: **Planning as an asset**. Planning can be an asset when you are tackling an inherited region or the task of expanding a business internationally, especially at the outset of your work. When you complete the planning stage following the guide laid out in the following pages, and you've finished your planning with prioritization of markets, you will know where you should spend time and money. I regularly run across examples of where a failure to plan leads to poor spending decisions, which ultimately produces poor results for the unlucky firm involved. The next pages will help many of you avoid common pitfalls due to proper preparation of your business approach.

Making a Useful Plan

Most of you reading this are bad planners. Don't take it too personally. Most people, including your chief executive officer (CEO), are bad planners. A personal goal I adhere to is if I walk out the door tomorrow and never return, someone could walk in and pick up where I left off. My desk might not be organized, and no one would ever figure out the chicken scratch in my portfolio, but if someone knows where to find my plan, business as usual could continue from where I left off. I always have a plan, and so should any businessperson with a strategic role in his or her organization's international business strategy. Most of you are saying to yourself, "Well, duh, of course."

You will need a plan if you want to approach your business development activities efficiently and want to leave a legacy of being organized. The job isn't necessarily any easier for whoever inherits it, because the same development issues persist. Even so, providing a clear road map to your strategy and thought process, and a layout of strategic and tactical implementation issues—not to mention some market background and justification of your efforts—is not only noble, but worthwhile, if you care for how your organization spends its resources. These issues tend to be equally important in both small and medium-sized enterprises.

Helpful Hint: **Visualization**. When I was an adolescent and playing competitive sports, I employed the technique of visualization. Once out of the batters box I could see that curveball spinning, see my body react, shooting my hips through the swing, getting my hands out front, and ripping a line drive right back at the pitcher. You could never visualize the desired result if you didn't have the fundamental skill to perform the task. I know there are nonbelievers out there, but you need to visualize where your business might be in five years and then in ten years. If you have lofty goals, then the learning curve and efficient market development should start at the beginning. A good plan is the start of the process. More importantly, beginner's luck and "bluebirds" (unexpected business) can only provide sustenance for a business for so long.

The reality is that planning is underutilized in all businesses, but especially so in international business. The only type of company that does not fit this stereotype is consultant firms like mine, which of course get paid to plan. If you are new to your field or your organization, you have much to learn about your business and the markets you may or may not enter. Even in the fortunate case where your organization holds an obviously acceptable or applicable product for introduction into international markets, you will need a plan to define and prioritize opportunities. You may be dumbfounded (seriously awestruck) by the sheer quantity of opportunities there are for your product or service in international markets. So how do you prioritize your efforts? Following a plan will keep you on a strategic path and away from allowing your attention to be diverted to unworthy opportunities.

I once had a boss who would sell our company's products to anyone who dialed his phone number or sent the general sales fax a generic request. Routinely he would drop anything and everything he was doing if some random reseller (not even a target customer or potential channel partner) phoned him about even a small sales opportunity. He would spend as much time as he could muster on the project. The mixed message he provided to the firm was convoluted. He'd socialize his random work efforts while simultaneously trumpeting the extent of work that we, his dutiful staff, were accomplishing to define strategic international business planning. This successfully diluted the message that the team was forming a solid basis for the needed internal support and buy-in to our international development strategy. Whether at quarterly sales meetings or a corporate Board meeting, he'd get up in front of the company decision makers and talk about how he received an interesting inquiry from Turkey last week and that it would now be added to his target list. Never mind the tens of thousands we were spending to develop strategic primary market accounts in Mexico, Canada, and Australia based on a logical ROI model. When he delivered this mixed message in my presence, my skin crawled, and I was embarrassed for both him and me.

This diatribe against one very flagrant incapacity of my old boss isn't shared in detest. On the contrary, he is a good man who worked hard, but worked badly as an international market developer. However, he was a perfect example of a tactical personality in a strategic position. He epitomized poor market development and faulty channel management. I think that for those readers who also may fall into the category of this old boss—that is, opportunistic and tactical rather than strategic—if you follow the following recommendations for planning, they will help make your business efforts more fruitful than they would be otherwise.

Planning Objectives

The objective in creating a plan is threefold. First, the plan should be designed to guide your development efforts for the short and long term. Taking even a broad brush to the international markets available to your business allows you to identify the market opportunity to justify your business. Establishing numeric and operational goals and a business case gives something to keep the eye on as a growth goal for the business.

Second, the plan should prioritize markets to assist in defining resource allocation for your business. Unless your business applies equally across the planet (though I'd have my doubts), a prioritization and implementation strategy should be made part of your plan in order to optimize the effort put into your business. Identifying the priority, secondary, and tertiary markets for your product is an underutilized outcome of the planning process. Once the markets are identified, they must be communicated clearly, and reinforced as necessary, to everyone in your organization. Setting expectations in business is always important, and the more you reiterate your strategy, the more likely it will sink in to those around you (remember, most employees are not international businesspeople and do not appreciate the compound nature of your efforts). I've probably done the prioritization presentation as part of a sales meeting to executive management ten times over the past five years. And that is on a formal basis. It is best to have consensus on where you are taking the business; you are less likely to be misdirected from someone above you if you make your strategy public knowledge in the company.

Finally, making a plan lends credence to the international venture to the executives at home. If a solid business case can be developed, high-level buy-in will be more forthcoming, and your job security will improve as well. Additionally, after high-level buy-in is achieved, corporate expectations of activities and results must be set so you can set and justify your performance levels accordingly. Who better to justify the criteria of success other than the person doing the planning?

Key Concept: **Before you get started, know your market.** Make every effort not to proselytize from the ivory tower, but rather provide realistic, market-based expectations built in to your planning process. This involves not only cultural/economic knowledge but also the ability to set initial business expectations (payback). Business models can differ markedly from country to country, and this understanding should be represented in the outcome of any well-based plan.

Sources for Planning

Sources of market research and data can vary by market, but typically you can get any plan structured by researching a variety of resources.

Secondary Sources

Traditional data research houses will provide market reports on any industry. Such companies as Dataquest, Gartner, and their peers create annual volumes on numerous fields that can provide the market basis for a given product or service history, demand, and future for any given region in the world. Because these reports tend to be expensive (generally hundreds of dollars for even the most basic industry report), consulting the sources' authors or editors for their recommendations can be a valuable process.

Other research options include the Internet, including sites like the CIA World Fact site,[9] Hoovers,[10] Wikipedia,[11] and various search engine sites. Internet searches are best used to gather market data information, rather than specific company information. Local yellow pages, libraries, and legal counsel offer other resources.

---

9   See http://www.cia.gov/library/publications/the-world-factbook/docs/profileguide.html.

10   See http://www.hoovers.com.

11   See http://www.wikipedia.org.

Primary Sources

A good second source of primary (firsthand) information can come from the major market players. This can be tricky, especially if you do not have market expertise or contacts, or if the major players would be eventual competition rather than customers. As you filter through the opportunistic individuals whom are interested in helping you grow your business, you will understand the level of value they provide as an information source. On the upside, however, confirming market data from a market player is an excellent method to confirm your own beliefs prior to making them a permanent part of an official corporate document that your name is on.

Everyone, everywhere in the world, will tell you success in business is largely due to your business and personal relationships with key market players. To an extent, this is true in Sweden, but it is much more so in high-context culture markets like Brazil. In a lower context culture, friendships are still important, but they aren't required for business. For example, I have a good friend in Sweden, but if he were to have left his post for some reason in the days I did business with him, it would have been relatively straightforward to continue the business relationship with the person taking his place. The same goes in the United States or other lower context cultures, but this rule doesn't necessarily apply in high-context cultures, where you must make a concerted effort to establish, maintain, and grow relationships.

Beyond the business aspect, it is nice to have some social contacts when spending significant time overseas. When building relationships keep in mind that you will get to know a certain strata of contacts. Based on the people you know and the interactions you have, you'll be able to horizontally build out business relationships in each market. However, just because you are well connected in Montevideo, don't expect to play golf with the president of Uruguay because you are in town for a business meeting. Relationships are interpersonal things, and so it is valuable to be realistic about the breadth and scope of your individual relationships. Always try to be aware of the extent and type of new relationships that you might be able to build over time as an extension of your current network.

Most importantly, you should focus on the relationships you manage to make and try and extend those relationships for both the long term and into new circles of acquaintances. In many newly democratic markets, powerful families ran business for generations. Whether you are trying to land a government infrastructure contract or sell widgets to the national supermarket chain, your contacts may very well know someone in your field business to introduce you to. With my breadth of close contacts in the major Latin economies, I can honestly say that entering and managing an entire new type of business in the region would not be intimidating, simply because of the importance and influence of my contacts. Imagine trying to say that in the United States!

Government Sources

Another fundamental source of information is the U.S. government. For example, the U.S. Commercial Service[12] provides a host of planning-related services. Outside the United States, the U.S. embassies or consulates are home to commercial officers. These officers, who I recommend getting to know for any market you start to do business in, can provide informal and formal market data, as well as establish formal introductions for your organization in virtually any market. The commercial officers usually bring with them an expertise in a given field. Try to locate the correct officer with expertise in your business area.

As with any federal agency, the assistance you receive is largely dependent on the talent and interest of the individual you deal with. The commercial service is home to as many entrepreneurial and helpful souls as it is to mindless paper pushers. Their support can be both domestic based and regionally (internationally) based. The Gold Key Program is one recommended resource. This program introduces companies with a market interest to prospective in-country partners. Note that most employees in the Gold Key Program won't necessarily have business experience (and if they do, it is very unlikely that their expertise is in your industry), so the program tends to be better suited for companies that are mostly interested in reducing expenses rather than ones more interested in finding the right fit or getting to a revenue stream quickly.

---

12   See http://www.buyusa.gov.

A US Commercial Service telecom officer in the Rio de Janeiro office of the U.S. Consulate was particularly helpful to me over the years. He would assist me to get introduced to certain companies I wanted to meet with and also provided me with occasional market reports. He created one report, in particular, that was timely and helpful in understanding the telecom environment in the wild deregulation days in Brazil in the mid-1990s. Although his expertise was on a macro level, his report nonetheless was locally based and gave readers a pragmatic description of events and the market. Due to technology limitations at the time, this contact was quite literally one of the few who could obtain the local knowledge necessary for the report. This point is still germane today, even with the striking improvements in technology infrastructure—That is, it is still important to identify and cultivate important contacts who can facilitate your entry into the local market. In fact I also now try to act as a resource to government commercial officials, in the hopes that a two-way relationship will be more productive when I require new or different information.

Helpful Hint: **Creative planning sources.** My firm recently worked on a consulting project where our client, a large information technology company working on a major strategy for their future global development, asked us to evaluate and provide market data on the Brazilian market. The information they requested was mostly about network ownership, Internet penetration rates, and the like on a city-by-city basis. This information was difficult to obtain from networks without local knowledge about Brazil. The client asked for some basic demographic and economic information about the same cities in the study, and we found that the information we received was all firsthand (from government officials and therefore extra-official) and that the Brazilian government only reports demographic data some three to six years after the time period in question. In other words, the most recent official data available anywhere was from 2001. It required significant market contacts and local market knowledge to be able to provide any data of value to our client. Sometimes you will need to be creative to find the information you are looking for to support your planning.

The U.S. Commerce Department employs international experts or regional officers who work from a regional office in the United States to assist the development of business in a specified country or region. These characters tend to range from world beaters to low-level bureaucrats who are paper-shuffling their way to an appointment overseas. Not to be trite, but some of these staffers, though they may provide helpful direction, lack international experience, true local market knowledge, and, even more critical, business experience. If the domestic group is the first you speak with for direction in a given international market, I would recommend confirming in the international market any information provided by U.S.-based personnel.

Sales agents can be a valid source for relevant market data if you have an agent sign on early in the development process (sometime this happens through ignorance or inheritance). Any agent worth his or her salt will be willing to start with a finder's fee, but if the information provided is valid and you close some business because of the agent's assistance, the finder's fee becomes a worthwhile expense.

Components of a Plan

A basic plan will include the following components:

• Executive summary: Do this as the last step in the written plan, but put it first in the chronology of the printed or presented material. It should spell out the prioritization strategy that was determined from the planning process, as well as other significant drivers (marketing mix, business model issues, and operational issues) in one page (the remainder of the report provides the detail behind the decision points). An executive summary provides enough reasoning to make a decision. The executives in your organization are highly unlikely to read your entire planning report, but they'll read the executive summary 100 percent of the time. However, they might not read it until you begin your formal presentation to the management team, so ensure that your key points and recommendations are concise and clear.

• Market background: What does your company do? Where are you in the evolution of your business? Why is it important you look at international markets, and especially these specific markets? This section should answer the question, "Why are we doing this?"

• Political environment: What are all of the political considerations that might affect your business? Are you evaluating a region or a group of specific markets? Are there political (trade policy, exchange rate policy, political philosophy, general population stability, etc.) issues that might impact your business outside of its home market? If so, you should know them, enumerate them, and make assessments based on the regions or markets you are considering. This section should discuss how the political issues you identified will impact your business.

• Economic environment: Describe the short-term macro and micro outlook as it pertains to your business. What type of economy is it you are evaluating? Is it a populist/socialist economy? Free market? Are there exchange controls, and if so, how might they impact your business, both in the markets you are evaluating and other markets you might eventually enter? How stable is the currency and the banking system? What are the taxation requirements? Integrate these issues into a coherent understanding of the markets you are analyzing. These items likely will impact your assumed business model and therefore your prioritization strategies.

• Relevant cultural issues: This is where you educate the reader about the demographic-cultural issues that might impact your business. Is the culture high context or low? Can you develop business in the evaluated markets from afar or is a local presence required? How does the local language or business customs impact your business there? What does that mean to your marketing mix and your business in general? If you are uncomfortable with this topic, hang on; I'll dive into more detail later in the book.

• Marketing strategy: Outline this section by market and include product, distribution ("place"), pricing, and promotion information for those by-the-book types who remember their MBA schooling.

Considering the relatively small body of work about international market development, there are an abundance of texts on the area of what can be classified as classical international marketing. Marketing at its core incorporates the four principles listed above. I recommend knowing the classical elements and their function and meaning from a general marketing sense. After all, in your home market, it is the classical definition of the terms (the four Ps) that creates the foundation of your business and product strategy. From an international development perspective, however, the four Ps and their application in a foreign market require special consideration with regard to the extension of your business in the international arena.

The "localization" of the products (which may also be services, depending on your business) that your firm creates and/or markets will require consideration. The object is to realize that the markets you are considering may necessitate modification of your product in order to make it relevant and even desirable to the market you are evaluating or actually entering. Small changes, such as language localization, labeling requirements, or other aesthetic attributes of the product itself, to larger changes, including major modifications of the product, where it is manufactured or sourced, imported from, and to, and support requirements, will require investment of time and money. So not only do these types of necessary changes need to be identified, but the cost associated with the changes should be part of your planning and implementation processes.

The channel(s) ("place") used to distribute your product may also need to be modified from that used to distribute in your "home" market. Distribution strategy, like product strategy, is many times an entire source of study in graduate management programs. Components of place include the method that your firm uses to get product to market—either directly (from the company and its staff on a direct or firsthand basis) or indirectly (via third-party distribution). Each of these methods has implications. The former may involve thorough consideration of establishing some regional presence to implement the business. The latter requires some ability of the home market to establish the indirect channels and then manage and support their integration as an arm of the home-market business. The logistics of distribution, or how your product reaches its new market, must also be considered. Is it different than the home-market setup? Do you ship from the home market or from elsewhere? What are the implications?

Pricing typically is more complicated outside of the home market. Part of your responsibility is to define, articulate, and implement the international pricing strategy. If you do this during the planning process, it can help you avoid potential critical errors in judgment later. Analyzing pricing considerations and including the assumptions in your planning directly impact your business' bottom line. Pricing incorporates issues identified in the other three P's. For example, international shipping or import tariffs are examples of price-impacting items. Others might be packaging requirements, incurred legal or administrative costs, additional product costs (either variable or investment), or channel margin requirements. Depending on how your business views such components, these items may be treated as part of the home-market overhead (less likely) or included in the profit and loss evaluation of the new markets (more likely). Therefore, the planning document is the right tool in which to define the pricing and margin impacts to the business in the markets you evaluate.

Marketing textbooks will tell you all about the reasoning behind the two more popular pricing methodologies, skimming and penetration pricing. Skimming pricing asserts that the company is basing its product price in the market based on the perceived value of the product, at as high a level as possible in order to maximize perceived value and margins. The opposite approach is penetration pricing, when a firm lowers the price to the lowest level possible, given the associated cost levels it may have in the international market, in order to achieve maximum volume sales and market share. Many times in international business there is a third rail to pricing strategy to mirror expected market practices for a similar segmentation, even if in a new or differing product area. This applies for a product where, because of the expected market response to the product, there may be a somewhat artificial elasticity to demand based on certain price levels, and thus companies are likely to optimize the pricing level to make their margin and volume at the maximum possible mix.

Promotion includes the effort to get customers to buy your products. Do you need to advertise? Is your product green (i.e., environmentally friendly)? Are the types of customers in your target market available in the markets you are evaluating? What medium should be used to deliver the advertising messages of your promotional strategy based on the market dynamics? Are packaging requirements different than those in your home market? How do aesthetics impact the promotional mix? Do you need to train your channel or your sales people? Is that different than what is done at home? How about channel support? Sales effort? All of these are items to flush out and incorporate into your international marketing strategy and especially your planning.

In most companies, the marketing of the products will actually be handled by other components of your organization once the planning is done and the business is being implemented. However, the person spearheading international market development needs to be able to evaluate the issues relating to a potentially modified marketing approach.

- Barriers to entry: Any of the above may be a barrier to entry worth restating, but this section of your report should identify not only the hurdles but potential solutions to implementation.

- Competitive environment: The international environment will be different than your home-market environment, and it is important that everyone reading your report understands so. Even your executive team may not have a good feel for the competition outside the home market. You'll need to educate them on the nature of the competition relative to your plan. For example, based your preliminary analysis, how do the home and international markets differ? Are there nontraditional competitors in the markets you are evaluating? If so, how should they be addressed? How is the competitive strategy in the international market different than the strategy implemented in the home market?

- Resource requirements: What will it take to implement your plan? How many staff members? What are the perceived travel requirements? Will you use inter- or intra-functional team integration? What are the operational considerations? Marketing issues? Much of your capability in this area will depend on your knowledge of the business and how it functions. Matrix management (managing across functional areas of the business) is often required for successful international market development efforts and should begin with the planning process. You'll need input from the other functional areas in your organization in order to properly identify and evaluate the issues important to your firm. Most importantly, you'll want to know incremental differences between today's home-market efforts and what you are proposing. How will that affect your company's current resource structure?

- Financial considerations: How much revenue and profit will the company make and when? Is the opportunity financially justifiable? Don't forget to list your assumptions. Know your firm's key metrics and how managers like to see financial data presented to key staff for decision-making purposes. Does the company make decisions and prioritize its efforts based on capital expenditure ROI, or is it top-line revenue? Sales per employee? Net income? And what are the revenue recognition and margin recognition issues related to your business in the countries you are evaluating? Can you repatriate profits? Does the home-market government have a tax treaty beneficial for your firm's business in the other market? Just as with the resource requirement section, enlist the financial personnel in your firm to get buy-in and to assist with the assumptions important to a proper financial evaluation for your company. Financials are something that may be modified or updated from time to time without too much of a burden.

> *Helpful Hint:* **Content is king**. The plan can be presented in any format acceptable to your organization decision makers. It is the content that counts. Make it easy to understand and decision oriented to best support your clearly defined objectives. Your planning needs may incorporate some, all, or many more issues than the fundamental ones described below. The structure and detail required by market or region will vary based on your planning needs, the complexity of your business, and (perhaps) preordained corporate planning strategies.

6
Developing Markets and Channel Development

The line gave off a spray of water as the arch slashed away, pulling the line straight back, away from the boat and toward the point where the yellow floating cord cut into the river. I lifted the rod tip toward the clouds and felt a yank on the rod's tip toward the river and the trout fighting for his life on the other end. Behind me the guide cackled his approval as he steered the small boat, bow headlong into the white-capped descent of the Valdivia River. I spun the ball of floating line taut around and around, finally getting the fish to battle the reel after holding the line taut against my pole in order to maintain the pressure against the small prince nymph stuck in the trout's lip. A few minutes later, I was swinging my fly rod toward the stern of the boat, gently coaxing the Chilean brown trout to rest in the guide's waiting net. I let out a triumphant holler as the best catch of the day was beaten, slowly shifting his tail in the net, waiting to be released back into the aqua blue river.

Later, sitting on the river rock bank eating meat sandwiches and gulping Crystal beer, I asked the guide about the color of the water in Chile. The aqua blue was unlike anything I'd seen anywhere else. I also asked him why the sky dazzled a bright sapphire, the grass shone emerald green, and the wildflowers seemed to radiate a Technicolor brightness to them. I wasn't drunk, and the excitement of the catch had worn off. Everything in Chile was bright and crisp.

"A combination of the copper in the water, lack of pollution in the air, and perhaps the fact we are at the extreme of the southern latitudes. And others say it is the hole in the ozone layer, somewhere near here, over the southern reaches of Argentina and Chile."

Well, I'd learned something new. And as I sat there, the roar of the river in the background, I enjoyed the moment, soaking in the sights, the sounds, and the experience of being somewhere new and learning something only experience could teach you.

I was in the south of Chile on business, because it was strategic, and the timing was right to help develop some business we'd been grooming for the past nine months. Valdivia, of all places, was the city I needed to be in at that moment in time, based on our planning and the priorities of our business. I had determined a few months prior that the best entry strategy for the market approach for our client was to start in the far outposts of the customer locations, build demand and interest and with financial results and then build the business back in toward its center.

When developing markets, due to the challenges of implementing a new paradigm in business, I recommend proving the concept prior to betting the farm on an implementation in the most desired market. For example, a regionally present company may be a target customer for a new technology or service. The possibility of developing that business into the headquarters market offers challenges due to the lack of desire to make autonomous decisions, delve from the standard quo, or take risks. Developing the business, instead, utilizing relationships established in outlying regions may provide a way to establish the business model and then backtrack to the headquarters market, allowing for ultimate regional deployment by the customer you most desired in the first place.

I enjoyed the fact that the moment seemed to culminate in catching a nice trout and learning about the river and more about the region that I would be working in tomorrow. I wondered if our clients would find my day as exciting as I had.

Owning the Developer Role

First, the person in charge of creating and implementing a market development and channel strategy should be familiar with everything else we've discussed in this text. As I mentioned earlier, if not you, then who? If you are responsible for planning the efforts, most likely it is you who is tasked with the plan's execution.

Assuming a plan has been developed, your plan will define where the priority, secondary, and other markets are. Based on the resources available to you, you can develop a time schedule according to a few of the following items: your short-term sales goals (i.e., how fast and how much revenue/margin), which markets have been okayed for entry, and any product development or marketing issues you have to manage to meet the requirements in these markets. You should have a clear idea as to what your plan is and the resources available to you, and then determine the time you will need to implement your market development strategy. Believe it or not, your strategic market development strategy will evolve into your tactical channel strategy.

Helpful Hint: **Time is not your friend.** Bosses want results, this quarter, this year, and maybe tomorrow. In the past, when I have asked clients to articulate their international development strategy, they always tried hard to describe it. What I have found is that there is usually a disconnect between the articulated strategy and its implementation. An example of this disconnect is a firm we've done some work for who wants to codevelop the large telecom wireless carrier accounts in Latin America and, simultaneously, increase distribution to retail accounts regionally across the Americas. The company sends its manager responsible for market development in the region on all sorts of wild goose chases to Central America and the Caribbean, when more time should be spent in the larger markets. Rather than wasting time (and money), they should be using resources to meet the larger potential clients and making ties to the influential retail distribution groups in Mexico and Brazil. Meanwhile, their marketing mix is not properly adapted, so the efforts in hopping around Central America is a waste of time from a strategic viewpoint. The shotgun approach costs the company tens of thousands in travel and operations costs (never mind the opportunity cost of spending time in nonstrategic pursuits), and the difficulty of following through in low priority markets is an unmeasured opportunity cost against what should be a more quickly growing business.

How can a poor strategy transform into a good one? Following are some examples of how this transformation comes about.

The former boss I referred to earlier (the one who pursued an opportunity in Turkey after receiving a phone call from a reseller) didn't have a written plan other than the one I had prepared for my markets of responsibility. He therefore considered all markets as equals. Strategically speaking, this may have well been the case. His market development strategy was simply to sell as much as possible in as short a time as possible. This may sound good to some extent, but not when you consider that you are not doing your job when you spend time dealing with the wrong markets. The resultant channel development strategy (the distribution channels you create and manage to get your goods or services to market) was a random, shotgun approach. We answered whichever phone rang the loudest and signed anyone and everyone up as distributors. It was utter chaos. It may seem comical to some extent in retrospect, but consider the consequences of such a disjointed and unplanned strategic approach to your international business.

Jump ahead one year when I was heading up the international sales efforts at the same company. Again, I found myself the inheritor of a few international direct customers, a handful of resellers (distributors), and a few manufacturer representatives across the globe.

The direct customers were fine to have of course (a direct customer usually means direct revenue and margins), but their profiles and mix didn't make sense strategically. I wondered why we had these particular customers, why we'd spent time developing modified product for them, and how significant their future potential was relative to the goals of the business and the resources we had to manage their needs. Direct customers invariably require significant account management attention, after-sales support, marketing resources, and face time.

The resellers tended to be opportunistic firms who showed initiative only after receiving a product information request from potential end-user customers, and so they tried to garner their market by pouncing on us when sales were presented. I can't blame the resellers for being opportunistic, but largely they were ill equipped to handle our business, and the management time required to hold their hands and go out and assist the business with sales would have made direct sales more appealing (and then again, this market would not have been a strategically prioritized market that we'd have spent resources on to begin with). You very well may be seeing a pattern forming here.

Occasionally it happens that even the most experienced international market development professional can use his or her skills and hit some dead ends relative to building new channels via new local resources. What I am getting at is the common example of the agent who oversells his or her capabilities. But in this case, it is someone you've vetted through your own relationships. That is, someone you've done business with provides you a contact that doesn't follow through or provide the level of partnership they've promised up front.

This recently occurred to our firm for a project in Brazil. We had previous contact and worked well with a Brazilian-based technology firm to provide us with some client introductions in various Central American countries. Later, after having success in building channels through their Central American contacts, we asked the same Brazilian firm for similar introductions into Brazil. They gladly obliged and made local introductions. Unfortunately for us, the company they introduced us to in Brazil started with strong interest, but then faded quickly, and the business ended up having to be started via another local firm.

The mistake made in this scenario was we took for granted our contacts' capabilities in their home markets. It wasn't that we had any experience with them in Brazil. We hadn't; so we made a wrong assumption. Our contact did not have experience growing a business in their home market. This would be like someone asking me for assistance with implementing a business in the United States, assuming that since I am a U.S. citizen I would have the knowledge needed, but not knowing my business experience includes little practical experience in implementing business in my home country.

Helpful Hint: **Vet your contacts.** The mistake of taking for granted your local contact company has been vetted when they actually have not been is more common than you might think, which is why I mention it in this book. Many times I have found myself in this position, even though I know how to sift through this very topic as well or better than anyone else. There was the time I spent too much time trying to determine whether an Argentine business partner's friend who managed a Brazilian company in Brazil could manage our interests in Brazil. I must have bought her and her partner three dinners, sent a dozen e-mails, evaluated her business strategy (for her core business), and on and on. She never followed through, never actually brought the contacts in Brazil to the table, and never did anything to actually help me. Then there was another instance in Panama when a local business owner and distributor for a larger company in a similar product space wanted to distribute our products. Even though this person and I ultimately became friends, from a business standpoint it was another lesson learned. I sent samples, made multiple visits, and spent time, money, and goodwill helping this person who evidently did not have the capability to implement our business. The products were different than the ones his firm carried previously, and his actual interest was to receive a quick commission that never materialized due to our inability to be successful.

Manufacturer's representatives are the most challenging to qualify and generally take longer to weed out (or formalize in) to the business. Representatives broker business for the company to customers, or in some cases from the company to distributors, who in turn market to customers. Either situation has business model and implementation issues for your firm to consider. Unless you have a wide base of contacts established in your markets of choice, a manufacturer representative can act as feet on the street to assist in developing a semi-direct sales effort or even establishing local distribution. Manufacturer's representatives typically seek a percentage of the business, regardless of who in the chain it comes from.

The biggest challenge in evaluating manufacturer's representatives or sales agents is that sometimes they bring intangibles to the table that may not be evident at first. For example, maybe they are in a related industry that currently sells to your customers. And even more likely, maybe they aren't. Determining the value they offer is often difficult. Ask for a business plan, a strategic plan, or a sales plan. Ask them to identify short-term and long-term product requirements for the customers in question. See whether they can identify the business model of your potential customers. Require them to provide professional references. These tasks can serve to both weed out unworthy representative partners and acquire good pieces of information that might shed light on their value in the business.

Helpful Hint: **The risk of contractual guarantees**. Most contract language allows for some wiggle room for both the company (vendor) and the distributor or agent to terminate the contract based on certain conditions of nonperformance. I suggest an initial contract of one year, with the ability to extend the contract based on a mutually determined performance level. A longer term contract may cause problems for the person responsible for cleaning up someone else's prior international channel development work. Resellers with contracts demand attention. It can take up to a year to end a contractual relationship, which can cost your firm time and money. At minimum, resellers are a preventable potential distraction from your primary market efforts.

Profile of an International Market Developer

The profile of a market development person is very particular, if not peculiar. It very well may not fit a description of you. The key is to acknowledge the key characteristics so that you will have the ability to identify your own skills and any other skill sets your organization might require in order to deploy its international effort. Even if you lack some of the skills, you can use the information presented in this book to manage the international market development effort of your firm. Being able to identify someone who might be able to assist you in your efforts might be just the lift you need to become successful at managing market development efforts.

For example, you may be an excellent communicator but lack

experience closing a deal. I fell into this category in my second market development job, where my responsibility included sales development. I had some sales management experience, but not with the volume of sales it was assumed I would be developing in the new position. Rather, to sell myself for the position I wanted, I sold my expertise in market development with a focus on business planning, relationship management, and marketing skills in order to put together a sound business strategy. This was all well and good, but I didn't have experience inking million dollar deals, which was what my new employer expected.

The way I muddled through this challenge was to enlist my management to assist in the sales efforts. They were happy to oblige, especially given that I was in a new subset of the industry in a new company. The sales support I got included picking the brain of the head of sales to determine how he approached selling our business to our domestic customers and then related this internationally. I even went to the extent of modifying domestic sales tools (presentations and the like) into Spanish and focused on my customers needs. I also used his sales proposals as a guide to what I was working with internationally. This approach had the added benefit of managing my international development with the related fundamental process that my senior managers had used stateside. I think this was a valuable methodology in establishing my own sales experience as well as gaining credibility at home.

Lacking some of the fundamental skills for market development can be real showstoppers. Two significant skill sets are the ability to communicate and the ability to adapt your development and business skills internationally. After you read the components of the skills required, it will become clearer that finding personnel with this variety of skill sets is no easy task. That is why there are MBA programs out there that teach some of these things! The difficulty in matching a market development position with someone with the required skill set to tackle the job is a common challenge companies face while trying to establish an international effort.

Business Skills

Possessing business skills mean possessing general business knowledge. Financials, marketing, and international business issues, like those brought up here in this book, are good to have when you embark on evaluating and developing your firm's international business. The good news is since your company has a home base, what you must most understand is your company in its home market. What are its products or services? What is the marketing mix? The margin requirements? The resource requirements? The operational requirements? If you have a good sense for these things, you then can use the guidance in this book to help you evaluate and implement your firm's global efforts. If you do not possess business skills, you will likely fail miserably at trying to fully comprehend, analyze, and articulate the intended international effort.

For the purposes of this discussion, business skills are a combination of general business skills and honed management skills. Business skills required for market development include the ability to read, understand, and analyze financial statements and metrics that are important to your business. This understanding, by default, means that you would have to understand the issues that impact your business' financials. Your understanding of personnel costs, infrastructure requirements, support costs, market and sales costs, etc., are all important to realizing success in international market development. When putting together your planning effort, as discussed in chapter 5, you'll want to include business modeling that incorporates variables pertinent to your organization's business in terms that other managers can understand and that correlate to what is going on at home.

Understanding and managing to your company's critical metrics (i.e., how success or performance is measured in the organization) will make you a better international development manager. In addition to general business acumen, your ability to think strategically and to assess opportunities in the international market is critical. Not just in general, of course, but specific to your organization. That is, you must be able to comprehend and articulate what the company must consider in order to properly engage your strategic plan and to implement business internationally. Additionally, an understanding of the matrix of functional areas (finance, marketing, operations, etc.) impacted by the implementation of the international development strategy is equally important.

You may be reading this book because your area of management responsibility includes international market development, but you may not be the actual person doing the work. You may have an employee, a team, or a contractor reporting to you who is doing the work. If you are the manager rather than the person implementing the strategy, you should be aware of your management methods and how they might impact the international development effort.

A person I worked for early in my career believed that locking in deals (i.e., signing contracts) was the only real measure for our success. Rather than taking a strategic approach to the business, by maximizing resources and revenue potential and recognizing the long-term potential value of new business—which is what the company's board of director's cared about in a public company—he took a shortsighted view to his responsibility for the international development of the business. This resulted in a less than strategic effort that focused on immediate results rather than the long-term international interests of the company. Longer term, not maximizing our international performance provided lower (albeit strong) returns for the business as it related to the company's strategic growth goals.

Sales Skills

Sales skills are the ability to identify, qualify, develop, and close business for your organization. Even if you have excellent marketing material and the greatest widget ever made, you will likely need some sales skill to recognize business from your efforts. There are many difficult steps in a sales process, including evaluating markets, identifying customers, qualifying customers, establishing a relationship, finding a need for your product, presenting a good value proposition, and negotiating a deal to close the sale. The most difficult skills to teach an employee are asking for business and making a decision to terminate a deal.

To create an atmosphere allowing for the possibility of sales, the ability to build relationships is key. It is the most fundamental sales skill necessary. Sure, the sales capabilities listed above are must-haves, but the ability to build a personal relationship is the foundation of building business in new markets. You may recall, from the discussion about cultural skills in chapter 4, that in high-context markets (i.e., most all developing markets) the ability to form and maintain strong personal ties with people is elemental to your success. In modern business vernacular, this is referred to as "relationship selling," "relationship management," or sometimes "solution selling" (or at least a key component to solution selling).

Relationships are built on trust, as is any friendship or kinship you might create in your life. Trust typically is built on actions rather than words, or on actions that follow up on words. Follow-through is a part of this, but mostly it has to do with building confidence in your ability to see something through that will create this relationship bond. When I discussed the business deal in Argentina in the introduction of this book, I alluded to the relationship that I had built with our client (who by the time the deal was secured was a friend). In developing-market cultures, unless someone can trust you, they are not going to entrust business to your firm. Therefore, building relationships is a requirement for sales success.

You may notice I don't mention the responsibility of the other side (i.e., your customer, your channel, your employee in the market or region) to help in the creation of a bond, or a relationship. The reason is that the market side has the relationship leverage. It typically is the market controlling the outcome of a given transaction-based relationship. Will the customer buy? Will the channel sell? Will the employee perform? They will be more likely to if they believe the other party (you) is a person of confidence and is a reliable source for their business, whatever it may be.

In international sales, closing a transaction may be different from market to market based on the cultural idiosyncrasies of the market you are dealing with. In Mexico, for example, I have learned that seeing (something on paper) is believing. In Brazil and Bolivia, a deal is done once the banks confirm payments are secured, regardless of the agreement in place. In Argentina, a written confirmation can in many instances be all you need to confirm a deal is imminent. In most of the EU and Canada, the rules of business are a bit more hard and fast (like those in the United States), where the actual confirmation of a deal is typically a formality. In all cases, the anticipation of closing and confirming a sale is the root of excitement for most businesspeople.

One of the things my students like least is my advice to them get some sales experience (of some type) during their career. In fact, it is virtually required to run any significant division of a for-profit company. And if you can find a CEO of any publicly traded firm without any sales experience, I will buy you a cup of coffee. Sales skills are essentially relationship skills that allow for a transaction to be created, for business to be done. For some reason there is a negative and ingrained hatred for the idea of taking a sales job after completing an MBA program. MBAs are supposed to be marketing managers, finance wizards, analysts, all of whom magically ascend to run businesses around the world without a spit of sales experience. Maybe it will make MBAs feel better if I explain that all successful business people sell. Investment bankers sell companies and deals, accountants and lawyers sell time and expertise, and a baker sells bread. Sales make the world go around and money flow. International business is not immune from the need for selling expertise.

Who in the organization is responsible for money coming in the door? Sales. Building the business? Sales. The relationships with your customers? Sales. Identifying the needs of the market today and tomorrow? Sales. Representing your firm to the market? Sales. If marketing is the lifeblood of the organization, then sales is the face, the personality, and the handshake. The person who is representing the entity. The one who brings the dollars (or the pesos or the yen) to the bank account. Most MBAs, with this inbred disdain for official sales positions, will find an alternate route to sales experience. Nonetheless, experience is critical to understanding your firm's role in the market how it functions in its own ecosystem. Sales skills are essential for being able to assess a firm's potential for growing its business internationally.

Marketing Skills

International market development personnel must have an understanding of marketing. In chapter 5, we discussed that the four Ps—pricing, place (distribution), promotion, and product—are a good start to defining the international marketing mix, because the person in charge of international market development is responsible for understanding and articulating to his or her company what the marketing strategy will be, or how it might need to be adjusted for international development efforts.

Pricing issues abroad are usually different than those in the home market. When a physical product is sold, it is either imported into the new market or manufactured there (based on your work in the pricing and product portions of your marketing efforts). In either case, the final product cost in the international market is probably greater than the cost in your home market.

Additionally, product issues, such as packaging and materials, and place (distribution) issues may influence the cost basis and therefore your market pricing. The market you enter may require direct distribution (i.e., the company selling directly to its customers), or there could be yet another layer of distribution as compared the home market.

International promotional issues can impact your pricing in many ways: essentially the pricing impact is directly dependent on how you plan to promote your product (your advertising budget, media selections, use of contractors, etc.). Just like in your company's home market, the market price you set in the international market will be based on the value proposition (the benefits your clients will receive by purchasing your product). The home-market value proposition plus the new realities of the international market may impact your ability to price appropriately to sell in a similar volume or segment in the new market. It is common that increases in the costs associated with the internationalization of your marketing mix may result in the business model not holding its same price/margin relationship upon which your home-market model is based. You may therefore have to alter your pricing strategy to be competitive in the international market. Ultimately you find that your value proposition in the international market is different than your home market and that your product or service won't fetch the same price. As indicated earlier in this section these modifications in strategies also may have implications to other components of your international marketing mix.

The ability to assess the marketing mix is essential to implementing your international market development strategy.

Communication Skills

All the effort in the world to support your international market development won't matter if you cannot communicate. You need to communicate with the markets you are trying to do business in. Your home office must be able to communicate with you. And you must be able to communicate with your home office about what is going on tactically and strategically with your development efforts. When I started 32 South, the driving factor was my ability to develop business in Latin America. What did that mean? Was I smarter than everyone who'd tried it? No. Was I a stellar sales person? Maybe at relationship selling; but still it was not the key to my success. Did I have the capacity to modify the marketing mix to fit our international strategy? Yes, with help from my operations and marketing managers. Was I able to strategize and plan according to my company's needs? Yes, but that can be replicated. Most important to my success was my ability to communicate, so that those other skills already discussed mattered.

You can understand and master 90 percent of what is in this book and yet fail miserably. You can plan beautifully, but unless you get buy-in at home, it is all for naught. Some of the components spelled out in this book may allow you to slide by without great communication skills. You might have a decent distribution strategy and be able to get it into place due to your contact network. But your efforts will likely be a lot more successful if you can communicate. Communicate to the interested parties. Communicate to your management what the development strategy is and why it is important to the organization that your strategy be followed (revenue growth, market share increase, profit increase, competitive move, etc.). Communicate to your functional groups how they factor in to the process to increase your chances of achieving buy-in. (You cannot do this all yourself, remember.)

You need to be able to explain to your CFO and your marketing director why the growth you are proposing is important and why their part in the effort is indispensible and what they and the organization will get from their involvement. Even if you have the highest level support in the organization, the implementation of your strategy will lag or fail if you do not get the right departmental support. You also need to communicate to your market why the acceptance of your business proposition is interesting enough to take on. Is your proposal compelling? Have you stated your case? Where is the value? Why should the market embrace what you are bringing?

Gaining buy-in through persuasive communication includes the ability to articulate your message in a variety of ways, including written, verbal, and physical methods. The ability to articulate means that you can relay a message and explain a concept such that the listener understands your point. Articulation of a concept is only as successful as its messenger's methods and the media used.

For example, sending a letter, fax, or e-mail is not a way to negotiate a contract in South America. E-mail may be okay for following up on a face-to-face meeting, to provide written information that corroborates your meeting points or to reiterate the products or services your company will provide to its clients. Raising your voice doesn't press the point in Mexico; rather, it is ignored as anger and does not have a place in proper business discussions. In many markets, writing a message in your native language would be more readily received than butchering the local language. Using an interpreter in places where the language is a critical component of the cultural identity is recommended if you cannot articulate in the local vernacular.

The capacity to build communication skills other than verbal skills is vital in international market development. Written skills are important. You do not want to come across as uneducated when you write something. Perhaps you have convinced your market contact of the value of your product and you intend to follow up with your contact via e-mail, with copies going to the other (and perhaps more influential) higher level contacts in the customer or partner organization. If you cannot articulate your message in written form (spell, and put together a coherent sentence or a cohesive paragraph), how will that come across? If you communicate poorly in writing, then you may lose some goodwill, or at least be knocked down a peg in terms of the management's perception regarding who their company is dealing with.

If you can put together an idea and articulate it both verbally and in writing, you are ahead of the game. But how do you come across physically? Do you make eye contact, listen well, make or avoid physical contact based on cultural norms? These items are all crucial, because physical communication affects how comfortable the people you interact with are in dealing with you! If they are uncomfortable, they may not want to watch you struggle through a presentation, a meeting, or a luncheon. There are ways to become more aware of the physical message you are projecting if you are naturally good at physical communication.

Most communication consultants will tell you that communication is 90 percent physical and 10 percent verbal. There is something to this—and I also think that the 90 percent is weighted because it is much more difficult to master than the verbal part! In cultures where personal relationships are more important for business the use of physical communication is also a key part of the communication effort. So your ability to communicate effectively means you need to be attuned to the physical characteristics of the communication in the markets where you do business. Just like learning the language, practicing your communication skills in market will allow you to gain a comfort level and be perceived, over time, as an effective communicator.

Helpful Hint: **Importance of language.** In addition to English, I speak and write Spanish and can get away with spoken Portuguese. Whenever I am in a country whose native language is Spanish, I speak Spanish in all business discussions. This includes presentations, meetings, during lunch, and on phone calls. I find that I am more quickly accepted when I speak Spanish in order to communicate in their home language. It is important that the attempt at speaking a language is thorough and not only for show.

When someone has made the immense effort to command a foreign language, the person on the receiving end of the communication is typically quite receptive of the effort. A mere understanding of the language understanding goes a long way toward gaining cultural acceptance. It is as if the people you speak with treat you more like one of their own, which then results in your ability to navigate the relationship more effectively and ultimately build your business more easily.

International Adaptability

Recently, while on a flight from Buenos Aires to Santiago, I sat next to a retired Argentine merchant marine. He had traveled the world during what I gathered to be a long and successful career. I asked him where he was headed, and he explained he was off to China for a month-long immersion course in Chinese. In his midseventies, he explained that his thirst for understanding other languages and cultures never abates. As a person who shared an interest in understanding global cultural differences, our conversation lasted the entire two-hour flight. Our conversation ran the gamut, but essentially we discussed the cultures and history of the United States, Argentina, and China. Topics ranged from the Louisiana Purchase to Argentina's protectionist agricultural policy that limits their ability to take advantage of a strong, global foodstuff market. It included the topic of trying to better understand why Latin American business and political cultures are so different from North American ones.[13]

As someone who had traveled the United States extensively ("more than I have my own country," he said), he was surprised at my knowledge of the Spanish language and of Latin American history and global issues. He said he felt that U.S. citizens have a local, insular view of the world, and he'd not known any who had firsthand knowledge of Latin American issues. I mention this story mostly because it was a fascinating discussion. And because he is right. I myself would have trouble having such a conversation with many people (at least business associates) back home, so I thoroughly enjoyed it. The other reason I bring it up is it is a great example of relating to or adapting to international cultural ties in order to really connect, and therefore do business.

International adaptability is the only real difference between a well-rounded business development person and an international market development person. A domestically focused business development professional is responsible for building business through creative

---

13   Jared Diamond. *Guns, Germs, and Steel.* W.W. Norton & Company, Inc., New York, 2005. [This reference is provided as the Pulitzer Prize–winning effort is a unique history of the world that offers an explanation as to why differing geographic and social histories explain cultural differences between societies.]

partnerships and selling products or services into markets where a company's interests are undefined and nonexistent. Building a business internationally requires the same tasks and then some. Don't get me wrong—the ability to adapt your business development skills to the international environment is not a natural skill. It is something that requires developing the set of capabilities spelled out in this book (cultural empathy, communication skills, business and marketing skills, and management skills), and then applying those skills to the international marketplace.

7

International Channel Management

I grew up in a small northern California town in a middle-class household, the son of hardworking Irish Catholic parents. My father was a California Highway Patrol officer, and my mother was a housewife and freelance writer. We spoke English at home, and only English was spoken in our town.

Later, in the 1970s and 1980s, anyone who spoke a different language was made fun of by folks. There was a rural farming community just to the south of our town that was heavily populated by migrant farm workers. Spanish was commonly spoken in the neighboring town. But in our town, we made fun of it simply because it was different, and we were a small town without a whole lot of outside influence. (In the late 1980s and early 1990s, the western United States was home to various legislation trying to outlaw anything but English as the spoken and written official language.)

In the early 1980s, my mother opened my eyes to the world beyond small-town California. She introduced me to my new pen pal, Clotilde, of Paris, France, daughter of Marie Therese. Marie Therese had been my mom's French pen pal since the early 1950s, when mom was a grade-schooler in Los Angeles. I wrote in English, and Clotilde in turn wrote in mostly French, though over time her English improved, and I occasionally added a word or two of French to my letters. It wasn't until I was in high school, when I actually started studying French, that I even dared to include some French phrases in my letters to Clotilde. I studied hard and found I had a knack for French.

Other than writing to Clotilde, I spoke French for a couple of months in 1988 when a freshman French student was in the same dorm I was in at the University of Arizona. He eventually quit speaking to me, because I knocked him out in a boxing match at the dorm. Later in college I opted for Spanish. I was living in Tucson, Arizona, close to the Mexican border, and Spanish seemed like a more reasonable pursuit than French. After all, I already spoke French, and I wanted to learn more about the language everyone was talking about in the press, at school, in town, and in legislatures, when discussing the future of American business.

What I found was that the root basis for the two languages was the same, and in fact, Spanish was therefore easier for me to learn than most. I rather simply allowed my brain to turn off any block toward accepting Spanish. The rules were similar to French (being a Romance language), so I accepted the rules and accepted the word and verb differences. I had laid down any impedance of picking up the language, and it worked. Later on I found that my ability to pick up Portuguese and to relearn a bit of French was also made easier by my ability to remove any perceived obstacles. Someday, when I am retired, I hope to hone my language skills much more.

While studying and learning Spanish, I was given a piece of advice by someone at school. A professor saw me struggling with science studies and suggested I study something I enjoyed. After all, he argued, you can go to graduate school to learn whatever you might really need to know in order to make a living. Soon after, I changed my major to history (with a Latin American concentration). My grades improved, and the fact that my Spanish dovetailed nicely with my history work made school much more educational. The fact that I was able to then pursue a graduate degree in international marketing solidified my skill set as someone ready to deal in international market development. And all along, doing something I enjoyed.

Channel Management

If you just accept that distribution (channel) management varies from country to country you'll be way ahead of the game. Coming to this realization takes knowledge built on experience. My experience includes fifteen years of dealing with different products in different businesses in dozens of markets all over the world. Cold, hard channel marketing theory is an area of traditional business study that just doesn't prepare you for the realities of conducting business throughout the world.

Recently, a discussion ensued after a question was posed by some of the most seasoned businesspeople I have known—why does indirect distribution work in South Africa but not in Chile? Both are emerging markets, are heavily dependent on natural resource commodities, and act as an economic and enterprise beachhead for regional business. Both enjoy democratically elected governments, after sordid histories of oppressive governmental regimes, relatively stable currency regimes, and substantial infrastructures. Chile, however, is smaller in population; business is centered in its national capital, and the direct presence of regional companies means they have a tendency to control their "local" business. South Africa, on the other hand, has a few important business if not economic centers (Pretoria, Johannesburg, Cape Town, and Durban), even though most Pan-African companies had their headquarters in Johannesburg. The spread of the economic base has evolved into a heavy reliance on indirect distribution and partnerships to build regional business.

Looking back, I realize that outside of the business concepts outlined in this book, the two skills I had going for me when jumping into this career choice were an ability to pick up language skills and some knowledge of Latin American history. What I didn't realize until I was already there was just how important these two items have been in allowing me to better understand what it takes to develop international business.

I cannot stress enough the importance of market knowledge before you take on the task of extending your marketing mix and implementing the international distribution of your firm's business. I think market knowledge is as important as distribution knowledge, perhaps more so, because it is less understood and not as emphasized. So many firms will try to force the square peg through the round hole and come up failing, without any indication that their complete lack of market knowledge and the market intricacies doomed the firm to failure.

Management Orientations

If you are reading this and you don't know much of anything outside your home market, relax; you are not alone. In countries where multiple language learning is not emphasized in primary or secondary education, there is not widespread appreciation for, or understanding of, the political, demographic, social, and economic differentiators between countries. This leads to what traditional international marketing textbooks refer to as "ethnocentrism," or believing that one's home-market cultural characteristics are superior to others. An ethnocentric management orientation occurs when decision makers eye potential international business opportunities through "home-market lenses." That is, their perspective is skewed by their tendency to evaluate "outside" business opportunities based on home-market values, cultures, and business practices.

After a decade and a half of international business experience, I can tell you that U.S. companies are viewed globally as largely ethnocentric in their management orientation. Based on my experience, Japan, China, France, and Mexico all tend toward ethnocentric views. An ethnocentric management orientation can result in all business decisions being evaluated on the basis of decision making back in the home market. However, speed to market, customer decision-making processes, margin expectations, and product reliability issues are all examples of things that might differ in an international market. When these issues are addressed through ethnocentric lenses, it lessens the likelihood that the firm will remain committed to its international expansion efforts. Using the same measuring stick for all sorts of business issues may also create negative goodwill in foreign markets.

The most negative application of ethnocentrism is "jingoism," when individuals actually look down upon countries outside of their own. An acute form of ethnocentrism, jingoistic tendencies tend to make the international expansion untenable, or at minimum, more difficult than it might be otherwise.

Other management orientations include polycentrism and regiocentrism. Polycentrism considers that multiple markets might share similar characteristics. In other words, it is a view that allows for differences or similarities between the home market and indeed between other outside markets. Regiocentrism treats groups of countries in the same perspective. An example might be Latin America, South America, the EU, Southeast Asia, Oceania, or the Middle East.

It is important to know your own firm's orientation as it relates to how you approach international business. Knowing your firm's perspective might allow you to manage information and business interactions in a way that increases your likelihood of implementing your business plan.

Knowledge of Supply Chain and Logistics

Channel management, or the physical and relational methodology of how your product gets to market, is important to understand in order to properly assess your business potential and business model overseas. Distribution is one of the four fundamental components of the marketing mix (recall the four Ps). Channel management includes managing the distribution channels that get your product to market, plus the logistics of required product movements. As with most business issues, channel management is typically more complex outside of the home market. Additionally, the international market development person likely has little or no experience in evaluating the movement of goods as it relates to understanding the company business model. Understanding the supply chain of your business will allow you to properly assess how the internationalization of the supply chain fits into your international marketing mix and your international channel strategy.

The supply chain, sometimes referred to as the value chain of a business, includes all of the inputs into a business in order to get your product to your customers. Components of the supply chain include product development, procurement (also known as sourcing or purchasing), manufacturing and operations, warehousing, shipping and logistics, and delivery. Each one of the points in the supply chain can be an element that must be modified dramatically, or not at all, when looking at international business.

Supply Chain Elements

- **Product development:** Depending on your firm's core competencies, there may be a geographic necessity for where manufacturing needs to take place. If country of origin details favor particular source markets it may impact where you locate a manufacturing facility or from which countries your firm sources components of a particular product. In either case, you should be aware of how product development activities are realized and how those activities might be modified for your international expansion.

- **Manufacturing:** Some country or regional markets have either local content regulations or tariff levels based on the product's country of origin. Protectionist markets (e.g., Brazil) are usually places where your product may need to be produced, manufactured, or assembled locally in order to be competitive.

- **Procurement:** Purchasing activities may need to be altered in order to parallel the production strategy discussed above.

- **Warehousing:** In international business the transactional terms of business may change based on a new or different method of distribution as compared to the home market. Your firm may need to change your warehousing relationships in your home market or identify new relationships to implement other potential supply chain modifications discussed above. Bonded warehouses allow for goods to be held in a market and be immune to taxes until the product is removed from the bonded facility.

- **Shipping and Logistics:** Delivery methods vary from country to country. Be sure to know when and how goods in your industry are delivered to their destination. Local vendors can be found most easily via your freight forwarder.

Effectively navigating logistical issues requires an understanding of operations (in addition to marketing). Over time I probably would have made a lot more money than I have if my knowledge of logistics had been better earlier on in my career. The overarching point here is that one should make a concerted effort to understand all issues associated with getting a product or service to the market of consumption. Several factors are at play that impact a business' bottom line, and I, for one, can vouch that this is largely overlooked.

The first element of physical distribution is getting your product to market. The markets you are considering may have a set of unique or at least different requirements that necessitate a product modification, impacting logistics or operations. For example, there are country-of-origin requirements for products to be sold into a market. As you do your planning, you will need to analyze origin requirements (i.e., where a product is built or finally assembled, or where it must otherwise meet content requirements such that the country of origin officially recognizes the good as an export). You may find during this evaluation that the types of goods your company produces and/or sells are more competitive when specific countries of origin are the source of the goods. Countries will have FTAs, preferential tax treaties, or protectionist tax regimes that dictate where a product ideally originates in order to make it more competitive and appealing to the market of interest.

Preferential Trade Arrangements

FTAs waive or at least reduce the import tax structure on a good. In NAFTA, goods originating from one of the three countries involved (Mexico, the United States, and Canada) are unencumbered from import tax when they are exported to one of the other two countries. Similarly, cross-border cooperation occurs with sub-assembling or designing of components, subsets, or final products, allowing unfinished goods to pass across the borders without incurring additional cost components from import taxes. Some FTAs are meant to be vehicles by which geographic regions enter into ongoing commercial or even simply formal relationships. A good example of this is the Association of Southeast Asian Nations (ASEAN) agreement, which started as a pact among southeastern Asian countries that looked to offer each other complementary products in trade, and then it expanded to enable regional political relationships to be formed or expanded.

Significant FTA areas include the EU, Dominican Republic–Central America Free Trade Agreement (DR-CAFTA), Asia-Pacific

Economic Cooperation (APEC), ASEAN, and Mercosur (southern cone countries of South America). Many technology products sold into Brazil at volume are manufactured to some level in Brazil in order to avoid the harsh taxation structure for imported technology goods, which many times will raise the cost level so high as to make the products uncompetitive. Once the product is assembled in Brazil (depending on the product requirements to achieve the country-of-origin certification), that good can be freely traded into other Mercosur countries, making the goods potentially more competitive within the region than they would be otherwise if imported from China, Taiwan, Korea, or the United States, for example.

Preferential tax treaties may lower the typical tax level associated with a good or service within a given market. Earlier in the book I gave the example of special arrangements between Chile and Brazil (Chile is not a full member of Mercosur), where in some cases a product or service may be levied a lower tax rate due to the special relationship, making products or services more competitive than they might otherwise be.

Brazil and Mexico have many examples of protectionist taxes in order to bolster national industry and promote local manufacturing, and occasionally to send a political message that otherwise might have difficult to deliver. In Mexico, for example, corded telecommunications products (phones and the like) have historically been penalized with a 129 percent import tax if the good originated in China, rendering such products uncompetitive. In Brazil, most all technology products are subject to multiple and progressive (i.e., one on top of the other, rather than on the base value of the imported good) taxes, rendering them unviable unless manufactured or assembled locally. Depending on your business product or service, you'll be better served if you fully analyze these issues as part of your planning process so that the business impact is known. In some cases, as described above, not knowing these issues can stop your business expansion dead in the water.

Once you have identified the source origin of your product or service, you can begin to address the logistics issues that impact your business. Build your logistics model from the basis of your product formation or manufacturer. Next comes getting the product to market. Whether you are shipping a toy on a boat from the Far East or are trucking a T-shirt from Mexico to Managua, there are business ramifications often overlooked by suppliers. If your company builds and markets a physical good that must be moved around in order to get it to market, one of the first resources you'll want to employ is a good freight forwarder.

Incoterms

It was only fairly recently that I determined my company was subsidizing high freight rates for a product to an international customer, and so to this day I evaluate the pros and cons of handling product deliveries from the international freighting extremes of Ex Works to DDP (duty and delivery paid) deliveries. International commercial terms, or "Incoterms," are the internationally recognized agreements to when a good's title changes from the seller to the buyer and are agreements international market developers must be familiar with. The most common transfers, FOB (free on board) transfers, occur when a product passes over the railing of a vessel or ship. Other Incoterms include picking up goods at the factory, known as Ex Works (from the dock of the factory), to delivering to the customer warehouse in the destination country, or DDP. All of the Incoterms[14] can be separated by their categorization of where the transaction takes place: at departure, at a point where carriage is unpaid, where carriage is paid, or upon arrival. The Wikipedia Commons graphic below is a decent illustration of the transactional differences between the various Incoterms.

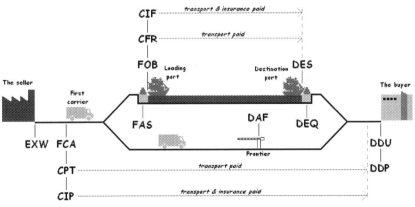

Incoterms 2000: Transfer of risk from the seller to the buyer

---

14   See http://en.wikipedia.org/wiki/Incoterm.

Most important, from the international market development perspective, is that each different transaction term has a different cost and risk impact on your business model. In each case, you should understand the impact it has on your business. For example, if a good is purchased from your firm FOB Port Hong Kong, it means your company is responsible to get the delivery to the port of sale and transferred to the buyer. If the good is purchased FOB Port Los Angeles (LA), then you may need to ship from your factory to LA, and coordinate your freight forwarder to transfer goods at the LA Port to the customer. CIF (cartage, insurance, and freight) means you are responsible for getting the goods to the customer's broker at the port of entry in the customer's country. The implications go on and on. If these terms are new to you, I recommend that you become familiar with them and even engage with a solid freight forwarder, who can walk you through the pros and cons of each method, help you determine what your transaction term options are, and most importantly, the implications of each to your business.

Freight Forwarders

Full-service freight forwarders move goods around the world. They pick up goods, transfer them to ports or to customer freight forwarders, manage shipment of goods nationally and internationally, manage warehousing including bonded warehousing, and even local delivery to your operation site or the customer. Firms will bond the freight forwarder, essentially giving them a power of attorney, to conduct transactions and be able to move the goods around for you. Freight forwarders are contract brokerage houses that interface with customs for export and import of goods and generally handle the logistics for what can be an extremely complicated process.

As the person responsible for getting the goods to market, or at least managing the information to include it in your business planning, you'll want to understand all of the steps needed for you or your firm's freight forwarder to get the goods to market. You'll need to know shipping estimates, transfer fees, warehousing costs, bonded warehousing costs, import taxation rates, brokerage fees, and any other related costs. These costs may be unique to your home-market model and therefore need to be included in your pricing analysis or business modeling.

A good understanding of delivery mechanisms and their cost structures enhance your business opportunities. You may find that your shipping or delivery mechanism saves the customer money. This means more margin for you or them, both positive scenarios. Your customer may be able to sweeten their business model to extend your business opportunity. You may make more money due to higher margins, or if there is price elasticity based on demand, you may in fact option to lower market pricing to increase sales. You can also set up logistics structures to handle unforeseen circumstances in the delivery of your goods or services.

Keep in mind that additional side products may need to be addressed when you evaluate this portion of the implementation of your business. For example, you might want after sales service handled outside of the country of service, or perhaps in-country training might be required for implementation for some period of time.

Distribution Hierarchy

Like the logistics and transactional issues your firm will evaluate, the type of distribution or channel management your firm engages in will impact bottom lines and may influence your prioritization strategy for your international efforts. Direct distribution is perhaps the most understandable method of distribution. It refers to a company marketing its goods directly—that is, without an intermediary. In this case the firm sells to its clients in the foreign market. The terms of sale may differ based on the business you are in and your clients' ability to manage logistics processes for their businesses. However, the management impact on your firm is significant. Direct means direct. It means your company is managing its clients, its marketing mix, and the post-sale support of your in-market business. Direct distribution means you have a sales capability in place and resources dedicated to implementing the business in a given market.

Indirect distribution means a reseller is involved. Your firm chooses, in this case, to sell to a third party, who in turn markets and sells your products or services in market. The implications of this include that the marketing mix, even if defined by the home country, is not controlled by your company. Another entity is your face to the market. Your firm is not directly managing the purchasing relationships in market, and so it is an arm's-length approach to the business. This does not necessarily mean it is a bad thing. As I alluded to earlier, depending on the business type and the country you are entering, indirect distribution may well be the most efficient and expedient way to develop business in that market. A company involved in indirect distribution usually has lower revenue than a direct distribution firm, simply due to the fact that the additional costs of getting the goods to market are incurred by another entity, and therefore the revenue share associated with selling indirectly is lessened.

Reasons for Selecting Indirect Distribution

- A product requires regular replenishment (high inventory turnover). Retail items are a good example.

- Local market knowledge about distribution or delivery methods is required to satisfy customer expectations. Examples of this are frequent orders and expectations for a short delivery time.

- You have many customers placing small (low volume) orders. Smaller transactions may be more difficult to manage directly, especially if your direct effort is transnational.

- Cultural reasons demand that a product be readily available for display, sampling, and training, all of which may be more easily managed via indirect distributors.

Whether a firm uses direct or indirect methods to implement its international business is not necessarily dependent on the size of the company. Some of the world's largest firms use some manner of indirect business management. Coca Cola utilizes independent bottlers, and Cisco Systems uses direct and indirect methods dependent on the market. Some other firms, like Hewlett Packard and GE, populate the planet with local operations to support their global supply chain. Some small firms may be better off evaluating their international market development strategy and then selling directly into key markets and using indirect distributors for low priority markets.

Key Concept: Direct vs. Indirect?

There are typical implications for managing business directly or indirectly.

Direct distribution occurs when a company owns and controls the distribution of its goods into a market. The key element of the direct model is control. Most importantly, a direct channel maintains control over the marketing mix. This means that the direct entity is likely to carry and properly market the entire product line, and manage its promotions, branding messaging, pricing strategy methodology, and commitment to post-sale support, including employee and customer training, accordingly. At the same time, there is a cost associated with direct management of the channel, so your firm will have to evaluate the pros and cons to going direct for your business.

Indirect distribution allows your firm to limit its direct investment in the market and to depend instead on local partners to provide resources to support your business' execution in that market. The negative to indirect distribution is a lack of control over the marketing mix. Reliance on a third party significantly reduces your ability to control product alignment, promotional support, brand messaging, price parity (or at least aligning pricing in a strategic way beneficial to the company's marketing and market objectives), and postsales support, including employee and customer training. In the case of indirect distribution, the home firm must still apply resources to managing the indirect channel. Further insight into this topic is provided in the Channel Marketing section of this chapter.

Sales Resources

The cost of managing a business directly is more costly than managing one indirectly. Indirect businesses (or those marketed through distributors of some kind or another) require the in-country distributors to invest in its ability to be successful. Training of its sales force, marketing force, technical force, etc., may include having to send its personnel to the vendor's home market. This is becoming less common, as many indirect business models include international distribution support of one level or another, which may include most or all of the training costs as part of the benefits the distributor receives in working with the particular firm.

Direct distribution companies must rely on a direct marketing and sales effort to build in-market business. This means people traveling abroad to evaluate markets, establish customer relationships, and manage in-market sales and support activities.

The human resources impact differs depending on whether you employ a direct or indirect distribution model for your international business. Indirect distribution means someone in your firm is responsible for managing the in-market partners. This typically requires less direct staffing; after all, the home-market staff does not have to be the ones running around the local market implementing the marketing mix— that is something your local partner are responsible for.

Post-sale Considerations

Even though this is part of your product marketing mix—that is, how your firm will support its service or product once it is in a given market—it is too often an afterthought. A firm my company performed some international market development work for was shocked when they saw we included in our strategy recommendations for what they should count on in terms of after-market support of their products, in terms of costs, contractors, logistics, replacement operations, and the like. The Chinese firm we were working with is one of China's largest consumer electronics companies, and yet they had entered another emerging market region without such anticipated evaluation of their post-sales business model. The result, I later learned, was that they were regularly flying product managers, technical engineers, and sales managers into the region in order to work out problems with their client, who had done their job and sold their million products out into all corners of the region, only without the proper support in place. These issues should be anticipated and included in your business plan.

If your firm opts to do business indirectly, then the after-sales component should be included in your local partner's plan, or your firm will have to find another local partner to properly vet, train, support (provide resources to) and incorporate into the planning model. If the business is done directly, the after-sales support is usually somewhat different than in the home market. In many developing markets, for example, customers don't have the same tendency to return products or ask for their money back for bad service as they do in the developed economies. The level of customer service provided is tied to the development level in a given market. Even so, for the post-sales support that is required, just like the rest of your marketing mix, it should be tailored so that it does its job. Do customers call in complaints? Bring faulty product back to where they bought the product? Know to contact or visit a repair depot? How does the exchange process work? What is the financial trail of such activities? Each of these may have some standard practices in the places you are doing business, so make sure to find out well ahead of time.

Distribution-Related Legal Issues

As noted earlier, indirect distribution means you have contracted with a third party to manage your in-market interests. Your firm has transferred title to the goods or service being marketed in the foreign location. Terms of the business arrangement, including the marketing relationship and the post-sales responsibilities, are passed from the home market to the indirect partner.

Your firm should have a contract (or multiple contracts, depending on the needs) in place to manage the indirect relationships that support your business model. Do you have a traditional distributor taking title to product? Is an agent involved in selling in-market? Do you sell to end-user clients? Does your firm employ a marketing firm for support in-market? Some entity is managing post-sales issues. All of these items should be governed by contracts. Ideally, contracts should be governed by the laws in your home market. If this is not stipulated in your contracts, it should at least be agreed that disputes will be settled by international arbitration rather than litigation. Your firm should call all the shots possible, since it is your business who is exporting its products and services.

For direct business, your home-market legal team needs to be more engaged than in an indirect model of business. If the business is direct, then like with the rest of the business, usually there is some matrix responsibility for functional areas. At least some input will be required on how things are managed, and at minimum there is *implied* responsibility. Your legal counsel may want to get local references, unless the international market development person can come up with the proper legal references through their own knowledge and contacts. The reason in-market legal counsel is required is because as a direct business, your firm has its skin in the local game. Ignorance to local laws, whether employment law, liability law, distribution law, or intellectual property law, is not a valid defense in the legal arena. All such laws come into play and must be understood by the home market since the direct business model is being implemented.

International Channel Marketing

We have already talked about some of the marketing mix issues (e.g., post-sales support) that are impacted differently based on whether direct or indirect distribution is implemented. You can't overlook the plain fact that virtually *all* of your international marketing mix may be impacted differently, depending on whether your business is direct or indirect. Channel marketing is how the marketing mix elements are managed into indirect channels. In other words, how the marketing mix is applied both indirectly and, in this case, internationally. The responsibilities within international channel marketing are numerous.

One of the product issues within international channel marketing is localization, which I touched on previously. Does your product need to be modified for the local market you are trying to enter? Are new or different features required in order for customers to be interested? Perhaps a different language is required on the product, or at least the packaging and user guides need to be translated. Are there local certifications or regulatory requirements for your product in your international markets? Is your international product strategy in alignment with the home-market product management strategy? If not, there most likely is some justification required. Finally, will your product need to be manufactured in a different location due to cost or import tariff issues? This bevy of issues is on the plate of the international channel marketing team.

Channel marketing also is responsible for promotional efforts into the indirect channel. These tasks are typically time and effort intensive in order to gain the proper mind share of your channel partners. Some of the activities include incentive programs. How do you get your channel to sell your product? Can you gain loyalty through an incentive program?

Incentive programs typically are based on either sales volume or product-specific volume. One of my favorite international marketing cases[15] is about CEMEX (the large, Mexican-based cement company) and its Egyptian channel strategy and the implementation and measurement of its incentive programs. The case-study authors indicate that incentive programs that are based on sales volume tend to be good in that they can get the indirect sales efforts more focused on end-customer needs. After all, whatever the customer wants to buy is most likely to be sold when the reseller is incentivized to sell as much as possible. There is a tangible benefit of the sales force listening to customer desires for product enhancements, which can also benefit the product development process. On the negative side, when sales folks (no matter where they reside) are asked to sell as much as possible, they are not likely to focus on the entire product mix or company marketing strategy, but instead on their pocketbooks.

The other type of incentive program is product specific. In other words, resellers are given financial or some other motivation to sell a certain number of specified products. In their case study, Martinez-Jerez et al go on to explain that product-specific incentives tend to direct the sales force to the company's priorities over listening to the customers' desires. On the positive side, product-based incentives motivate the sales force to educate customers about the product mix. This can motivate the channel to focus on value-based selling, which can leverage future benefits of selling premium or differentiated products. The result is more likely to be increased loyalty of market customers in the long term. And similar to the volume-based incentives, the sales force will bring back product feedback that might help in the product development process. Finally, using product-based incentives helps the company plan inventories, forecasting throughout the product mix, etc., as compared to the sales volume based incentives, which may tend to introduce chaos into the planning mechanisms of the business.

Channel marketing must also manage the implementation of any price discounting, including rebate programs. This may require setting

---

15   F. Asis Martinez-Jerez, Joshua Bellin, Carole Winkler, "CEMEX: Rewarding the Egyptian Retailers," Harvard Business Publishing, Cambridge, MA, 2006.

up tracking and measurement methodologies, depending on the rebates and the conversion rate of the rebates.

Advertising programs, whether implemented by the company or via its indirect channel through cooperative marketing programs, are coordinated by the channel marketing team. Advertising may be controlled by the home-market branding or promotional teams and farmed out to local contractors for implementation, or they might depend on local contractors to implement via a direct relationship. More common in distributed goods, a company will ask its reseller to manage advertising efforts via cooperative advertising.

Cooperative (or "coop") programs typically instruct the in-market channel partner to implement advertising activities, approved in advance by the company. Approved expenses are then tracked and paid for via a credit that is typically accrued as a coop advertising line item, and is a percentage of distributor purchases from the company. In the high-technology sector, coop programs vary from 1 to 3 percent of sales. The company channel marketing activities should include defining the coop levels, defining the approved types of advertising, including content, and monitoring and tracking the coop campaign and credit system between the company and the distributor.

Helpful Hint: **Have a home marketing mix established.** If you are one of a rare breed and starting your business and your international strategy simultaneously, marketing mix issues are of utmost importance. If you do not have a home marketing mix established, then the international application of the marketing mix may end up driving your domestic marketing variables, so you have to be careful. As long as you and the firm have priorities and goals, then the marketing elements are more likely to stay in line against those strategic concerns for the business. The product elements, build requirements, support requirements, and features must be flexible enough that when the internationalization of the product is done, it doesn't negatively impact the firm's ability to introduce what is likely to be the core home-market product strategy. Similarly, efforts in terms of managing the distribution, the promotional plan, and the pricing must be conceived in a way that the home-market (assumed to the be the key market from a revenue and margin standpoint) strategies are not irrevocably altered in a way that makes managing multiple approaches to the marketing mix (domestic vs. international) difficult.

International Channel Marketing Management

Another component of channel marketing is the management of the channels themselves. I introduce this concept to ensure that the international market development person, who may well be responsible for channel marketing as well, since in many firms they don't distinguish between the responsibilities. If a firm formalizes its international channel marketing position as separate from the market development person, there are a few tasks that should be done in concert. These include selecting the indirect channel partner, determining who manages which elements of the channel management, and determining communication efforts and methods, along with training, support, and other marketing mix implementation issues. A more traditional marketing person will have a valuable opinion to how each of these items should be addressed so that they are in alignment with the home strategy. Balancing what is best for the development efforts as compared to the alignment with the home strategy is something that will have to be determined by the involved players based on the company's priorities.

The channel marketing manager will likewise be responsible for the pricing elements of the international business. Again, alignment with the home-market strategy is an important consideration. Some cases will allow for an identical pricing *strategy* to be followed. In most cases, however, companies will go to market with varying prices from market to market. As discussed in chapter 5, some variation of skimming or penetration pricing typically is employed by integrating the home-market strategy in the context of the other issues that might impact foreign-market pricing.

Margin analysis is also performed as a component of the channel marketing mix. To be done correctly, this requires the input of the international market development person. As we've already learned, there are so many aspects to the international business that it necessitates the international market development person be involved in setting international pricing strategy. I can recall almost exclusively being involved in evaluating pricing strategy and being responsible for margin analysis regardless of my role in the organization, be it marketing, sales, channel management, or some other role. The person who is responsible for the international implementation should also perform the margin analysis.

As described in the planning section of this book, the modifications required for your marketing components may be different depending on how your service or product is distributed. Pricing and product issues also will need careful consideration and will depend on the distribution method selected.

8
The Distribution Beachhead

When armed forces invade a territory, the first thing they do is establish a beachhead, allowing them some physical ground to set up headquarters. They use the beachhead as a launching point, communications center, and equipment depot for their military efforts in the area. Without a beachhead it is virtually impossible to create a concerted effort in the new country. Imagine the Allied forces effort in World War II in mainland Europe without the D-day operation and their establishment of camp at Normandy. There would have been no western push to meet the Russian and Allied forces from the East, and VE Day might have been postponed, at best, and never happened, at worst.

Businesses starting in international business do so as a result of a number of impetuses. It might be a well-thought-out strategy and planning justification that starts your efforts (if so, you are among a select few). More likely, a business development manager in the domestic unit received a "bluebird" opportunity (a relatively easy business opportunity to implement that provides unplanned revenue) to make a sale to an international customer (usually it is the customer who deserves a good amount of credit for making a bluebird deal actually come to fruition). The reason the formation of your initial international business strategy is important is that how you arrived at your decision to establish a beachhead will affect your initial strategy and might provide you with different challenges in approaching the task.

How do you know which market is your beachhead market? It's initially a tough and seemingly esoteric question; but with a quick analysis of your planning efforts, the answer typically is clear. The concept of managing the business from a beachhead strategy again lends credence to the planning requirement discussed earlier in this book. If management can be shown that your decisions relative to the management of the business efforts are based in planning and sound judgment, your credibility will be increased, and the management team will be more likely to listen to your advice.

Getting out your planning document, make a reference to your priority markets as you've identified them. That is as far as you need to go. Usually a beachhead market will be a single country market, but it also could be a close-knit economic region where one sales, product, and distribution strategy will satisfy the business and cultural requirements for the block. Portions of the Caribbean, or the countries of Argentina and Chile, might be good examples of a multicountry bloc that makes up your beachhead.

Your planning document should note the priority markets as the ones with the largest revenue and margin opportunities coupled with the most manageable development or product resource requirements to meet those goals. The market where you expect the 80/20 rule to apply (80 percent of your revenue and 20 percent of your customers) is most likely your beachhead market. Remember, the beachhead is where your odds of success are best!

Leaving the military comparisons, the beachhead provides your business with a likely revenue stream—revenue you can count on, providing future cash flow that will inevitably be the piggy bank used to fund any resource requirement you might encounter for managing your international efforts. Company management will generally make each business unit responsible for generating the operating revenue needed to support its efforts. The odds of the international division being allowed to be a long-time loser are slim to none, so count on either creating a beachhead with an expected revenue stream and related contribution margin, or rethink your commitment to the international effort.

Without an expected revenue stream and expected cash flow, your business efforts will be in a constant battle of resource pinching that will consume management time and career capital. It may not be a battle worth fighting for you or your company. If you spend your time in management meetings reviewing budgets, budget modifications (likely cuts), then modifying planning expectations and forecasts, you will have less time to have feet on the street to actually make your revenue numbers. Eventually, the lessened revenue will require you to either have deep pockets (this of course assumes the proposed payback for additional investment is sound business practice) or management's deep faith in your efforts to manage the business without a beachhead.

In addition to avoiding resource problems, a beachhead can provide the boost you want and need to grow your business. The beachhead, with its more solid expected results, allows for resources for additional development of your other primary markets and possibly your secondary markets. In other words, it is what allows you to begin more extensive implementation of your business plan.

Allow Time to Understand Your Business

When I started a position as director of Latin American sales for a Southern California high-technology company, I assumed I was going to get to use all of my learned international market development experience to grow and manage a stable distribution business. After all, I had recently come out of a position managing international marketing (what turned out to basically be a market development management position, where I was responsible for setting strategy and managing its implementation), and so I felt ready to take on a larger market responsibility for a more established distribution business.

Of course, two weeks into the new job, I knew just how wrong I had been. It really only took two significant efforts, learning the market segment of the product line that we were selling, and reviewing the sales reports for the last twelve months (some of the current distributors had been in place for eighteen months or more), for me to realize, quite plainly, that this was a "turnaround position"—one with no history to even ascertain whether a turnaround was plausible or even possible.

What's interesting relative to the beachhead issue, however, is that the idea of the 80/20 rule is so pervasive in business that management was certain where they thought they should have business, even though the business hadn't yet come to fruition. Given the fact that the beachhead hadn't yet panned out, coupled with the fact that many would-be secondary and tertiary markets had already received significant attention (and so required more attention), I knew I would be spending the first twelve months of the job assessing what I had, traveling the region, putting a plan together, and cleaning house, even before I could get to the concept of establishing a beachhead (assuming the markets warranted my involvement in the first place).

I think I spent about 80 percent of the next twelve months on the road, traveling to Mexico City, Caracas, Sao Paulo, Rio de Janeiro, Campinas (Brazil), Santiago, Buenos Aires, Lima, Panama City, and Puerto Rico. It was during this time that I experienced the searing heat of Brazilian summers that happen to fall at the same time as U.S. winters. Unfortunately, the business casual fad didn't hit Brazil until the 1990s, which, in retrospect, seems strange since Brazilians are the most casual people you will ever meet in your life. Nonetheless, the result was that I was wearing wool suits in the summertime in Sao Paulo, sweating through meetings, and ruining a few suits over a very short amount of time. I can recall getting off the plane in Brazil and my eyeglasses immediately fogging up and being amazed when Brazilians ordered coffee to drink at meetings. All I wanted was cold water or cold beer, and not necessarily in that order. I remember driving along the beachfront streets of Rio de Janeiro and looking at all the bikini-clad women while I baked in the non-air-conditioned taxi in my black, leather-soled dress shoes.

These trips were when I got my feet wet in many of these markets. It was when I let customers order for me, and I ended up eating cow glands in Uruguay and marinated cow heart in Peru. Both are delicacies, but ones I ate only once. It was also during this time that I trekked to wineries in Chile, spent a day on Impanema to soak up the Brazilian sun (although my first experience resulted in severe sun burns as the sun's power in the Southern Hemisphere is much stronger than at home in California). It was then that I learned where to stay in an inexpensive hotel and where to pay for relative safety and comfort. Also during this time I toured the major cities in the region; I tried all of the food, the drink, met the people, and made some friendships I still maintain to this day.

It wasn't until later in my next job (two years later) that I started to create relationships in these countries that would truly form my career. Relationships that would facilitate my business dealings in these countries for years to come. What tends to happen is that as you work your way up the responsibility ladder in Latin markets, the folks in charge (the owners, the executives) tend to stay in charge—even if they are not in the same companies or industries—and will forever be invaluable to your ability to affect business decisions in these areas.

Categorizing Regions

In my experience, Latin America can be broken into categories relative to their business behaviors. These subregions are as follows: Mexico, Central America, the Caribbean, northern South America, Mercosur (sans Brazil), and Brazil. These six fairly distinct areas in most cases are a grouping of countries where shared experiences resulted in similar histories, demographics, distribution and financial systems, and cultural similarities and led to similarities in buying behaviors. Mexico and Brazil tend to be outliers in most regional categorizations. Brazil was colonized by the Portuguese, and the inhabitants developed a strong, unique culture tied to its Portuguese roots, with a fantastic native cultural and important slave influence. This was followed by further European influences over time, and up to the period of its independence. Mexico was the first mainland colony of the Spanish in the region north of South America. Dubbed "New Spain" by the Spanish colonists, Mexico was an important region in the Spanish colonies. Strong native and Spanish cultural mixes, coupled with Mexico's need to deal with its neighbor to its north, have contributed to a unique business history. The other four subregions can be loosely grouped due their similarities.

The Central American "banana republics" experienced a similar historical focus on local economic activities, and individually the countries have found niches in natural resource economies. Extreme poverty for the masses and a strict class system has allowed a significant separation of wealth, still evident today throughout the region. Still, this neighborhood of tightly associated countries has resulted in strong ties in trade, logistics, politics, and economic associations. Regional corporations are commonplace, as are regionally defined marketing and distribution strategies.

Northern South America, or the northern Andean region, is mostly comprised of Peru, Colombia, Ecuador, and Venezuela. The smaller markets of Suriname and Guyana don't get much attention simply due to their very small populations and subsequently small influence on the business issues of the region. Agriculturally oriented, these markets have epic histories involving native populations and their conflicts with colonizing Spaniards. Ultimately, all three countries embraced decades of authoritarian control and military dictatorships, subjugating the poor native populations in a social position that fomented ultimate revolt and institutional changes. More recently, the pendulum has shifted to socialist tendencies in Peru and Venezuela, although the Peruvians are showing signs of fighting that urge. Colombia, one of the bright stars in recent Latin American political history, has battled internally with a rebel war and infamous drug cartel problems, only to embrace democracy and enjoy growth during the years President Uribe was in office. These markets, though somewhat unique in their own right, are adjacent to each other and share a kinship of history and culture that allows the three to largely be considered a unit when it comes to assessing business issues regionally.

Mercosur (a free trade zone including Argentina, Brazil, Uruguay, Chile, Paraguay and Bolivia, among others) has learned to fend for itself in the context of the world stage. Geographically isolated (Chile and Argentina are as far from New York as London is from South Africa), these countries each have an economic reliance on themselves and those close by them. Politically, like much of South America, a long history of post-colonization military dictatorships plagued the region, typically delaying industrial progress until the late twentieth century. Chile, of course, is the diamond in the rough. With significant annual growth since its democracy took hold in 1990, Chile has integrated the world's best examples and is an open economy, highly technologically advanced, and extremely competitive, and therefore consumer friendly. Argentina continues to suffer from politically wrought economic angst, making it a difficult place to do business. Exchange controls are tight, and taxes on the movement of money severely limit both foreign and domestic-to-foreign investment. Avoidance of interest payments on the International Monetary Fund debt has put Argentina in a precarious position relative to the world financial markets. Paraguay and Bolivia are smaller markets and have experienced greater levels of native population oppression that has left their economies a few paces behind others in the region. Uruguay's population is small but relatively successful. All of these markets speak a related type of Castilian-based Spanish.

The Caribbean is made up of many countries of varying histories and economic focus. Much of the region is dependent on tourism, although a few of the markets have large enough populations to demand more economic attention. The Dominican Republic, Puerto Rico, and Jamaica are the leading business markets in the region. Though Puerto Rico is part of the United States, it is more similar to Latin America from a business standpoint.

9

Evaluating Direct Market Presence

We stood at the chest-high bar in short sleeves with beads of sweat lining our foreheads and dripping down our necks. We were in the dark wood paneled Santa Catarina, a hotel in Minas Geris, Brazil. We toasted each other's health and our future partnership with a shot of Minas Traigo, the local preferred *cachaça*. With a harsh cough and through tear-blocked eyes, I blindly searched the bar top for my beer chaser. After washing it down, I was able to smile and shake hands with Danilo and Claile to cement our impending deal for my company to buy their company, manufacturing facility, technical know-how, distribution channels, and all, for a long-term payout that stood to make both men very wealthy. I recall looking out the humidity-fogged, second-story window of the old, hardwood-paneled bar onto the lush, coffee-covered hills and wondering what they would spend their money on in this one-horse town.

Earlier that day, the hot, four-hour ride from Sao Paulo to Santa Catarina was only supposed to take two hours. The constant potholes in the road were only one reason for the delay—the other was the distance. We stopped at each road side store for cold water, Guaraná, or Gatorade. Time estimates should always be doubled in Brazil, and I knew better than to expect two hours, especially in the summertime when the locals want time to go faster during the sweltering February afternoons. Maybe if we'd been in a helicopter it would have taken two hours. Danilo was driving fast, like most Brazilians who drive like they are chasing down the memory of Ayrton Senna (a Brazilian race car driver and triple Formula One world champion who died at the wheel of his car while leading the 1994 San Marino Grand Prix). The conversation at least was colorful, as it always was in Danilo's company, so the four hours felt more like three. We slowed down as we approached the destination. The town had no stoplights (not one), and only a couple of stop signs to slow (not really stop) traffic at the corners of the cobblestoned streets. We pulled into his company's headquarters (and manufacturing town) to meet with his partner to lock up the deal for my company to purchase his in order to form a long-term strategic alliance and local presence in Brazil.

When to Go Local

There are always unique factors that must be considered in each particular market when determining whether to establish a local presence. In my experience (twice in Canada, once in Brazil, Mexico, Argentina, and South Africa), each case was different in its reasons and eventual justification for establishing a local presence. In any case, management must identify a strategic reason for *considering* the market, and then must further identify a reason for *evaluating* the market as to whether or not to enter the market locally. It may be that your beachhead business is growing such that local support is cost-justified rather than continuing to finance the extensive travel required to support the market. This is the most frequent reason managers even consider going local. If a significant amount of your company's business is coming out of a particular market, as a keen business person you will ask yourself whether more attention should be paid to the market or whether the existing resources are enough. You may wonder whether you are nurturing the local business enough.

Helpful Hint: **Who's the decider?** In many cases, the idea of a local presence in and of itself is intimidating. You may think, *who am I to push for some international presence? I just manage the international sales for this particular area.* Or, *I am only responsible for business development for this region; who says I am in charge of creating a local presence?* If not you, then who? Even if your company has a mergers and acquisitions team, in all likelihood you will be responsible for setting the business case in motion prior to someone else actually handling the formalities of any deal making. It is common that your company's counsel and executive team will be involved throughout any process of establishing a local presence, but don't be surprised if you are the one responsible for justifying and leading the process. After all, you are the person ultimately responsible for the success of the international venture.

Extent of Local Presence

The extent of the local presence you choose to implement is relative to the size of the business (i.e., the capital available to implement a foreign operation) and the expected return for the market chosen to establish a presence in. How your firm goes about establishing a local presence depends on which of these two drivers impact you most.

If the parent company has a large pool of working capital, you would likely argue for a foreign presence based on the business case and the potential for growth. In other words, if business planning demonstrates high potential for a local or regional business, the parent company is likely to lay out a larger investment to ensure that the local entity is established properly. In this case, "properly" means using tried and true methods of establishment where legal and financial risks are well understood, defined, and assessed up front vis-à-vis the type of establishment created. There are firms that can be contracted in the home market to establish a firm's presence in Prague, for instance, in a way that offers the least risk to the home firm. Of course there is a cost for this level of expertise. It is worth mentioning that if a firm utilizes this approach, it can realize greater returns (there is some efficiency to scaling this out globally) if utilized more than once, because in theory the cost will lessen, relatively speaking.

Keep in mind that internal resources of the firm are still required when utilizing such an approach. Attorneys still need to sign off on actions, as do Boards, CEOs, operations managers, and others. Ensuring that the firm is setting up the business the right way the first time theoretically minimizes risk and helps deter extra costs down the road, when things might have to be done differently, or a second time. Alternatively, firms that are big enough may want to utilize their own internal resources to implement the international presence. This means using inside (or contracted) attorneys and other personnel to determine the right way to implement the business. Companies with extreme global expertise (i.e., multibillion-dollar companies) may well have the infrastructure in place and the economies of scale to justify this work. Otherwise, it will be an easier learning curve and less expensive to use a professional services company. Larger firms looking to establish a small international presence will likely be more careful to not "overdo it." Either of the two methods mentioned above will enable the establishment of a more limited presence.

Smaller firms typically will base their approach to establishing their foreign presence on the expected ROI. If the firm expects an enormous return and has an executive team committed to the planning expectations, it may opt to utilize a professional services firm to establish a local entity that covers their needs both short and long term. If the expected return is less than huge (relative to the home-market returns), the firm is likely to utilize its own resources to establish the presence. These resources can include its home-market attorney, who would then find the proper legal referrals to get opinions to then determine the course of action. A second option is for the marketing/sales/operations organization to get in-market attorneys to provide direction. The more difficult task in this approach is the in-market attorneys utilized may not completely understand and appreciate the expectations that the home market attorneys or accountants might have.

Helpful Hint: **Future impact of local presence**. Once a decision has been made to establish a presence in a foreign market, it sets in motion a series of market realities that severely change how you might address that market in the future. The impact of a lasting enterprise is less of a challenge to fully understand than the impact of a failed or aborted attempt at market entry. I worked for a company that had pulled out of the Canadian market only weeks before I came on board. The company had opened a direct office in Canada to manage its sales and support efforts north of the U.S. border. The office in Canada was staffed with a few employees who acted as a local branch office of the company. Business had halted due to technical problems experienced with the primary products being sold into the market. Some time later when the firm had addressed quality problems and was ready to reengage the market, the lingering negativity from the historical problems were such that the likelihood of generating additional revenue from that particular line of products was nonexistent. Firms should try to account for how current business decisions might impact future maneuverability in a market.

Decision-making to Establish a Local Presence

Assessing the feasibility of establishing of something new to support your expanding business is always a challenge. Occasionally the reasoning is clear. Perhaps your firm is new, and the home-market business has been established to simply test the waters for international expansion. Maybe your home market is extremely competitive, and you feel you need to look outward for survival. It is also possible that your business is so large that to maintain growth for growth's sake you desire to look outward.

In 2007 I was approached by a former business associate to establish a new business in South Africa. My friend was successful in his own right, having established and sold off successful businesses of one size or another in England, Bolivia, and Chile. He approached me with a business model that was not yet implemented but was well tested by him under different businesses in different countries. Based on his knowledge of the business model and the background research he conducted to determine priorities, he was convinced that South Africa would be the best point of entry for the business. Upon receiving the planning document he developed, I read it with interest and a bit of skepticism. Some might think it is easy to take an idea successfully implemented in one emerging economy and implement it with the same success in another, even halfway around the world, but from my vantage point, a bit of skepticism was not only prudent, but necessary.

As it turns out, my friend had done his homework. Although the layout of his strategy varied from that recommended in this book, the essential elements were there. I was so impressed by his work that I agreed to pass it along to potential investors, who considered the deal. After some overseas flights and further corroboration, four of us sat down over dinner in Silicon Valley, California. At one point, one of the two primary financial investors spun his wine around his glass and asked, "Kevin, would you invest the money?" After I said yes, he responded, "Well, that is good enough for me. I'm in." Then the other investor chimed in with "then I am too."

Looking back at the analysis, discussion, and decision, much of it was based on the principles presented in this book. My friend had a thorough understanding of the business issues and a good understanding of the business culture. He also provided a reasonable explanation for the prioritization strategy. As presented, it turned out to be a valid investment proposition for a significant angel investment that might well lead to a significant and market-altering business entity in the African communications industry.

Beyond creating a well-defined concept to enter into an international, rather than home, market, the push of competitive pressures may well direct your firm into international expansion. Today, as our African business experiences its initial stage of growth, we are considering expanding the business or its products into other African or emerging markets. The timing of such an expansion is key. Half a year too early and all the advertising money in the world won't save you. Half a year too late and significant global players are bound to have considered an entry.

Most of the time, expanding a local presence in a foreign market is something considered only by larger companies that have a history and an already-existent global or at least important home-market or regional-market share. These companies, for one reason or another, look to expand internationally to gain a competitive advantage and to survive. Staying at the home market, given today's global economic situation comprised of interrelated exchange rates, banking policy, and channel ubiquity in flat market countries, really allows easier expansion of market players into new competitive markets. Therefore, the home-market company very easily nowadays can be pushed into additional international markets to gain market share or to establish a competitive advantage to survive.

Another reason to look outside of your home market might be because you are a relatively large home-market player and need somewhere else to build a market to grow and create prosperity for the business. This is typically considered by a regionally significant business rather than a single-market or global business. Why? Because a single-market business may not have a strong market outside its home market, and a global business is likely already established in the places in which you are thinking of expanding your business.

Depending on the reason behind your decision to look at international markets, you should fall back to the criteria laid out in chapter 5 in order to properly evaluate, prioritize, and implement your firm's growth strategy for its international presence.

10
Managing Your Interests Back at the Home Office

One topic I haven't spent enough time on in this book is the importance of constantly knowing the temperature of things back at the ranch. While you are out running around the world trying to build business, do you know if the boss is still buying in? Probably you do to some extent if the company is still paying your travel bills! All kidding aside, international market development is an emotional drain on any company—it takes a lot of physical and mental energy to carry off building your international business. There is nothing more potentially damaging to the international developer than getting the rug pulled out from under him while in midstream. I experienced this once firsthand.

One of our European clients knew very little about doing business in the Americas, and we were contracted to set up their ability to buy data services from major service providers in the region. That part, although a challenge, was easy enough given my experience in dealing with the technology industries in the region. However, the European firm created an internal, unrealistic expectation for growth on the sales front in the region without providing much in the way of additional resources. Eventually, once it became clear to their management team that revenues were going to be slow in coming, coupled with the fact we'd done the heavy lifting of setting up regional vendors to provide them their lifeblood of data services, we became less useful to them, and our contract was severed without notice.

In retrospect, from a business standpoint, it is difficult for me to blame the firm's ownership. I harbored some animus against them for some time after the severance of our development contract, partly because they didn't see through the terms of the deal, but more so because they didn't appreciate the relationships we brought to the table that then had to sever without the proper notice. It was a classic example of how *not* to manage development in the Americas. More importantly, it solidified the lesson that without full knowledge of the interworking of the home office (they were, after all, a contracted customer and several thousand miles away), we stood little chance of ultimate success because we didn't participate in any management discussions regarding their vision for the region. Finally, it was a lesson in making sure that the home-market firm fully understands the responsibilities they have in making an effort at developing international business.

The development person ideally will maintain close ties to his or her home office and to his or her management (or to those holding the key to the kingdom) and will understand the current and future role of the international effort, at all times. Anything less is a recipe for failure and could impact your regional relationships. And remember, it is the developer who must bridge the gap between high-context cultures, where relationships are important to business, and low-context cultures, whose management many times are not as empathetic to the needs of building relationships in high-context culture business markets. Although our firm's personal relationships persist after explaining the nature of the pullout to our regional contacts, I am sure our previous client's business in the region will have a significant cooling off period as a result of their decision-making. The two specific courses of action that will help you maintain the right relationships back home are to know your boss and to understand the fundamental management metrics of your business.

Know Your Boss

Knowing what your boss is thinking is important. Your boss, in theory anyway, should be the one leading the international effort. If your boss is a board of directors or the senior staff of an organization, you may have even more work to do to keep tabs on their awareness of your efforts and how those efforts and the strides you are making are viewed at the home office. Being able to anticipate your own priority requirements in managing your business is a valuable asset. Should you be focused on building a beachhead? On improving margins? Entering new markets? Cutting costs? Building a better team? If any of these is the case and you were not aware based on your own assessments, you'll have to get the information from those above you.

Your boss may not hold the purse strings. Most likely the strings are held at either the senior staff level or the CEO or Board level when it comes to international development efforts. Since international business is a foreign effort, it is almost always considered a new venture, and the company's board of directors will need to approve the investment and strategy modification before okaying the pursuance of the international effort. There is legal reasoning behind this—decisions of this nature need to be made in the "light of day" and with gravity. A public company will have to answer to shareholders, and a private company might need new capital to support the international venture. These reasons and many more mean that the company must officially buy in to the effort, and thus Board must approve any action and will monitor its progression.

If you answer to the CEO or the Board, getting their ear and attention will be part of your normal (or abnormal) routine. If you answer to anyone else, it may take some extra effort to make sure those groups setting the corporate strategy are aware of what your efforts entail. In one position I had, where I was responsible for the international effort but was two levels away from the CEO and three from the Board, I was able to not only make presentations to the senior staff, but I volunteered putting together presentation material for Board meetings, which I did; as such, I was able to get a debrief on the reaction to the material and the discussion that ensued. I was therefore always up to date on the thinking and direction of the Board. It worked beautifully to keep me updated on the perceptions of those in charge of the purse strings.

The Metrics of Your Business

Like all of us, your boss and his or her boss manage to expectations. All you can hope for is that those expectations are (at least eventually) built on solid metrics that are understood throughout the company. Metrics, or numbers of measurement, vary greatly between companies at many levels. Some numbers are more important than others, depending on your firm. Revenues and margins usually are important no matter where you work. Investment, working capital requirements, bookings, cash flow, ROI, the number of customers, gross margin, contribution margin, EBIDTA (earnings before interest, depreciation, taxes, and amortization), and even net income after taxes are examples of important business measurements around the world. Your firm may assign more importance to one than the other or may measure your international business in an entirely different way. You'll want to know what metrics are important to your firm's core business and how those metrics might apply differently to the international approach. Then you'll want your planning and management expectations to be based in metrics that make sense as applied to the international endeavor.

11
Avoiding Common Missteps

The toughest part of assimilating all of the information presented in this book is knowing which information is important to your organization when considering your international development strategy. Does it matter that Hugo Chavez is implementing "business unfriendly" practices in Venezuela[16] when your business is about to launch its South America operations in Chile? Probably not. So don't spend time focusing on matters not important to your business.

Information is everywhere nowadays. You need to know what to look for—what type of information might impact your business. Once you know that, then knowing where to look to find it is an easier step. Information gathering is essential from the beginning of your responsibility, since from the moment you start, a lack of key information could be detrimental to your efforts. It can hurt in two ways: when you don't know something you should, and when misinformation derails or impacts your ability to implement your plan. The latter can be damaging to both your project and your career, and the former can impact your project and your reputation in your organization.

Let's say you work out your planning for your firm and make your recommendations for strategy implementation, which are then followed and implemented. If you made a rudimentary oversight because you didn't know the pertinent information to lay out your case, then you

---

16   "Venezuela Extends State Control of Oil," www.cbsnews.com, June 26, 2007.

are negligent in your planning responsibility, and your planning had a faulty basis.

An easy example might be not having cultural awareness of calendars and seasonal work flows related to how they impact a project's implementation. If you have a twelve-week build schedule for a plant in Brazil and you start your implementation clock on December 15, you probably will finish your project in two to three times the projected timeline. Brazil virtually shuts down over the Christmas and New Years holidays. Then Brazilian employees take mandatory summer vacations in January, and Mardi Gras is invariably in February each year. By mid-March, most Brazilians are back to the grindstone, working up their momentum for projects in April through July of the year. When your project pushes out and it is clearly a management error, guess who is responsible and why? You! Because you lacked information—information that is readily available with the proper due diligence in your planning process.

The second category of misinformation—for example, when your company CFO asks you about the Chavez government in Venezuela when you are focusing on Chile—can be handled well if you know the facts about the lack of Venezuelan influence in the Chilean economy. You also might be well off to know the political structures in play and the fact that Chile has been stable both economically and politically since Pinochet was removed from office in 1990. When your planning allows you to deflect such potentially damaging assessments by your co-workers, you protect your plan and yourself from embarrassing positions. What do your co-workers necessarily know about the topic? In other words, if you don't properly address your CFO's contention, then you will look the fool even if she is not correct. However, if you have conducted your due diligence, your colleagues will perceive you as knowledgeable about the region and will feel more at ease about your running the company's interest relative to the business in the region. This may lead to that CFO asking for your opinion on a range of topics regarding the firm's international interests.

I could write an entire book about the pitfalls involved in international business, but like most things in life, learning by your mistakes is a great way to move forward. I found out about a company near the Silicon Valley area that has a hot new product that apparently is going gangbusters in both the United States and United Kingdom. The founders were American and British, so the reasons for starting in these two markets are as plain as that. It happens that their flagship product is a nice fit for these markets. But that is not the case when it comes to their international expansion.

The impetus for their particular international approach is based on multiple factors. First, by ownership their business concern is a multicountry company. Second, their product idea (a green industry) transcends geographical boundaries—a marketing segmentation that transcends borders. In lay terms, their primary product is something that has a segment of users not only in its home market but in many markets, across cultures. So the advocate of green technology products in Utah is as likely to want to buy it as the green consumer in Montreal, Paris, or Athens.

After the company gained some steam (it was generating cash flow to fund expansion and even pulled in outside investment to increase penetration in its key markets), its founders and Board naturally wanted to expand the business outside its key markets. Keep in mind this is a company whose transcending nature has done business in many "flat" countries of the world. What was pulling them out of that sphere was the fact that even emerging markets were becoming green-oriented. Of course, the challenge, from a product perspective, is that the high-end (high-priced) product is not sellable in the emerging market, as the value proposition is not such that a reseller would finance the purchase of the consumers, regardless how interested they might be. Therefore, the grand idea became to develop an emerging market product that fit the need for a green product, especially when this product actually would help the poorer societal segments to a) save money on household expenses, and b) provide them with access to more technology services as a result of the use of the product. Finally, they were able to develop a version of the product that met the economic needs of the emerging markets. So now what to do?

Well, of course they wanted to sell it in the emerging markets. But where to start? Without relationships in place and without significant experience in such efforts, they hired a couple of talented marketing people to lead the charge into business development in emerging markets. So far, after twelve months, little strategy has been formulated, and the last I heard from their Americas manager, he was heading to El Salvador and Mexico next week. Now, El Salvador and Mexico may be longer term markets for the product, but neither is a good short-term market based on many reasons. For example, neither market can be developed and implemented quickly for the type of product under consideration. Creating channels for a new product segment is a time-consuming exercise in developing markets. Second, El Salvador has a more fragmented distribution system than the United Kingdom or the United States, and identifying an obvious channel partner for a market approach to a green technology product is not clearly achievable. Next, Mexico is not green—far from it. Finally, El Salvador has small potential, relatively speaking. I could go on, but this handful of reasons would be enough to keep me away.

A formal market analysis of these markets, or even just a rudimentary plan as proposed in this book, would save this company a good amount of time (quicker to revenue) and even more money (money spent more efficiently to produce results). Many times in a case like this, and not unlike others my consultancy has encountered, the firm would be better off prioritizing very difficult but large potential markets (Brazil, South Africa) in parallel with implementing their business in a more accepting market, albeit one with less potential, to test the implementation strategy (Uruguay, Panama).

Cleaning Up

Another typical task when taking up the international market development responsibility for the first time is cleaning house. No one likes this part of the job, but it is almost always necessary. Of all the time I have spent in international business, probably a third of it has been cleaning house one way or another. Keep in mind that cleaning house cannot be accomplished without the aid of planning. If you've planned, what needs cleaned up is more obvious, because you've likely identified it as part of the process. Which market is taking marketing resources and not producing revenue or margin, or is not even on your priority market list? If you have one, it probably needs cleaned up. Which market has underperforming distributors, untrained representatives, legacy agreements that don't fit your current partner profile, or even customers who don't pay and require more support than they offer in positive cash flow? All of these cases needing some maintenance, and most times I recommend creating a clean slate to work from.

Cleaning up someone else's mess, where the local entity (customer, distributor, representative, etc.) is beholden to a previous regime or strategy in your firm, is likely going to take more effort than is appropriate. I have brushed this topic with very broad (maybe too broad) strokes, but in fact, the topic of international channel management and all that it entails requires a book of its own!

12

If It Seems Too Good to Be True …

We'd been sitting inside because the wind was whipping up along the river out on the patio outside. The tablecloths were trying to jump from the tables, and silverware was clanking on the concrete slab floor. The wind, as it is known to do occasionally in Buenos Aires, was pushing the people indoors. We'd received our drinks, and I took a long swig of Isenbeck beer, which was cold and bitter on my parched throat. After landing from an overseas flight not two hours earlier, I was tired, thirsty, and had a headache. I wondered to myself whether these were symptoms of the voyage or preparation for the conversation that had just begun. "The ownership has decided to make a change." Thirty hours of travel for one sentence to be said face-to-face, man to man, the way it needed to be done in this part of the world.

Eighteen months earlier my business mentor and I met in a small Los Gatos, California, pizza joint. The place was hip and lively, with exposed brick walls and metal ducting on the two-story ceiling, framing in the louder than desired music and the scuffle of the hipster wait staff decked out in black trousers and tight, white-collared shirts. After the iced teas arrived, he told me he had a business project he'd wanted to share with me. He was old friends with the CEO of an Asian telecommunications service provider. The publicly held company had done what they could to grow a profitable business in Asia and parts of the Middle East. Latin America was next, and they wanted a partner to help them find the way.

My mentor, a retired technology entrepreneur and now an "Angel Investor," a financier, ran the concept by me and asked me two things.

Was I interested? And where (which country) do we start in? I was interested but needed a couple of weeks to answer the second question. My firm evaluated all of the major technology consumption markets in the region, and for various reasons we ultimately selected Argentina as the logical starting point. Fast forward a half million dollars in equipment, cash, and resources, not to mention the opportunity cost. We had funded and ramped up a competitive service provider in Argentina, only to see it barely get off the ground, failing miserably.

Once we had selected the market, I used my local contacts (which were substantial) to determine the logistics involved in getting the business off the ground. The plan that was created was clear—purchase a company with a license, make the proper governmental submissions, hire a lead person who was capable to build the local team and implement the business, and do it all in concert with our Asian technology partner (later a financial partner, and what was probably an exit strategy for the investors).

What we did incredibly wrong, and I take responsibility for it, was we hired the key local executive based on the knowledge of our local business partner rather than vetting the selection through a third party or a truly knowledgeable source. In fact, the one other senior executive who had known the fellow we'd hired asked me, "Why'd you hire *him?*" I should have known right then and there that we had made a mistake and looked harder at our decision, but we were rolling, money was being invested, and the executive we selected was working hard.

It wasn't for some time, until the pain of the problems of getting the technology to work properly surfaced, that the ownership team realized the team put in place to implement the business was the wrong team. This team had created a faulty marketing strategy, and its execution was questionable. All told, it was a complete and utter waste of time and money.

Looking back, the lesson learned was brilliant—no matter how skilled one becomes in expanding international business, in order to be successful, one has to have a successful home-market business that then must be tailored accordingly for international expansion. With our entrée into Argentina's voice over Internet protocol (VOIP) market, we knew enough to select a market with the right kind of potential (difficult as it is to build a business in Argentina), but we lacked specific knowledge of several key business issues that would have helped us in the first place. These issues included the expansion and acceptance of the technology we were dealing in, a full understanding of our business model, managing personnel issues in a foreign market, and properly implementing a channel marketing strategy based on a proven home-market marketing mix.

Technology and International Expansion

Technology is an intriguing tool to utilize for an international expansion.[17] Researchers Joanne Roberts and Chipo Mukonoweshuro studied the use of technology and its use by South African banks for international expansion. The idea of geographic expansion using technology as a basis for product and growth is largely based on three factors: first, whether the firm owns the technology and considers it a core competency; second, how "locational factors" influence the capacity for international expansion (in other words, depending on what other capabilities, including information communication and technology (ICT), exists there geographically to support your firm's efforts); and third, whether the firm has some relative experience in utilizing the technology as a driver for growth. Finally, the importance of "psychic distance," how nearby markets may act relative to the uptake of a particular business, cannot be underestimated. (This is a theory I am a big believer in, and in fact write about in layman's terms in chapter 8, when I refer to the similarities between the six identified Latin American regions that allow for regional separation and expansion.)

Back to Argentina and our VOIP business. Regarding the three factors presented above in the South African banking example, we had the technology as an ownership capacity (factor one), but only to a point. One of our investment partners was a VOIP carrier, so we had some global technology, but we did not have an excellent grasp over the VOIP technical deployment in Argentina. Locational factors (factor two) were an assistance to us only in that we had solid business experience in Argentina. We did not, however, have local ownership

---

17   Joanne Roberts, Chipo Mukonoweshuro. *Digital Technologies and the Cross-Border Expansion of South African Banks.* Hershey, PA: Idea Group Publishing, 2005.

experience in Argentina, which was probably strike two. Our business had experience with the technology (factor three), so this was not simply a hit or miss proposition. So all in all, we had approximately 1.5 of the 3 necessary factors to successfully utilize ICT as a means of international expansion.

Even though I am translating this academic research fairly rigidly, I think my comparison has merit. If I look at what we learned from the Argentina experience and compared it to my company's recent undertaking in South Africa, here is how we fare. We have good experience with the technology due to the ownership group's experience in South America (remember, the other party at the table had executed a successful strategy with the same technology in Chile). Second, we certainly do not have locational expertise, but what we do have is a clear profile of the market as it compares to our combined experiences in South America. Assuming the developing markets act similarly, then the localization point is largely addressed. Third, our business experience with the technology is quite strong. So all in all, we register a solid 2.5 to 3 out of 3 of the necessary factors for success, and so I am hopeful this bodes well for our future in South Africa.

Grasp of the Business Model

While this is a premise to basic international market development, it is more critical when considering a local presence in a market. Since the risks associated with having the wrong model are perhaps a wasted direct investment, the reasons to ensure that your business model is sound are therefore quite important. In the two starkly different scenarios presented above, relating to our experiences in creating a local presence in Argentina versus South Africa, our understanding of the basic business model was one of the great differences. In fact, from a planning perspective, our financial skills were significantly stronger in Argentina. Of those of us directing the strategy, the ones responsible for reigning over the numbers until they were right were all quite experienced in this sort of thing. What was missing, of course, was the business model experience for this specific business in this type of a market. We could model numbers till the cows came home, but without the proper expectation of the right variables to include in the model, our planning was indeed fatally flawed.

In South Africa, by contrast, the financial mind responsible for the creation and management of the business modeling is not a financial mind by trade by any means. However, we knew quite well the business model aspects and their relative importance, we knew the pricing strategies that should be expected with the segmentation we were to approach, and because the business was in fact well understood, the business modeling task was more manageable. So even though the numbers require occasional tweaking, the business model is fundamentally sound.

Personnel Requirements

Just as is mentioned in the South Africa banking case discussed above, one of the great challenges in South Africa is the selection and retention of qualified staffing. I think this is one of the great challenges of the lesser developed countries by and large. In 2008 I spoke at an ICT event regarding general ICT deployment and societal/political/economic issues. My portion of the event was more humdrum, as it was about the actual penetration rates of broadband access technologies in Latin America.[18] More interesting, however, were the constant comments from senior managers from some of the worlds most influential ICT firms about the lack of human capital development in Latin America and emerging markets. In other words, the humans in these regions need more resources and support in order to create a better educated and skilled workforce, who then can contribute to the betterment of their societies, both from an ICT deployment standpoint and otherwise.

In Argentina, we relied on the skills of a family businessman without the proper ICT and business management experience. He lacked the ability to strategically lead the organization in a way that provided us the business model and marketing knowledge necessary to survive. However, it perhaps was much less his doing than ours that we suffered great ills related to the technology deployment, as discussed in the section previous. To lay blame properly, the principal shareholders (me included) should have placed one of us with serious skin in the game and business management experience on the ground in Argentina to

---

18   Institute of the Americas, ICT Outlook 2008 (www.iamericas.org).

run things. The outcome, although the cards were somewhat stacked against us, might have been different.

Unlike in Argentina, one of our cofounders is on the ground in South Africa to direct our new venture there. He is our CEO and is driving the business. Other than perhaps the quality of the technology we are deploying, he is our greatest asset. Our greatest challenge has been a lack of qualified staff for key positions. In fact, it may yet be the cause of our demise. However, with some luck and a few more key staffing assignments, our business could be wildly successful. Staffing is that critical, and is that much of a crisis.

Marketing Mix Elements Related to Direct Market Entry

I don't imagine that the marketing mix is any more rigidly controlled and implemented as it is when a direct presence is being established. Depending on the investment involved, it may be that the time to success must be shorter or the venture risks failure (due to the increased cost structure). Should your firm have limitless pocketbooks and not be in a rush, however, direct presence probably provides the best possible chance of a complete marketing mix success. With a local presence and local employees representing the interests of the company, the company can gain local knowledge that then can be turned into efficient and strategic decision making regarding product issues, pricing, promotion or, distribution challenges. In Argentina, we ran out of time to take advantage of these possible positives. In South Africa, I am hopeful we will gain strength over time.

In summary, direct presence should be considered for the right reasons. Just believing you have the significant market experience and a smart home management team does not guarantee your success. But if you consider the technology implications of your business, if you know and have a tested home-market business model, and if you are able to get the right local team in place, you only have to be able to withstand time in order to implement what can be a more insightful and efficient marketing mix for success in a foreign land.

Afterword

From the front yard of our home in northern California, I can look out over pines, redwoods, and oak trees and can see the land that I grew up on in the distance. I, and now my children, have endured endless days of hiking the trails through the oak chaparral, thick with stretches of poison oak, scrub brush, and blackberry bushes, hunting for snakes, trying to catch a glimpse of a bobcat, and loading up on wild boysenberries until our fingers were stained purple-black.

Today though, the view is different. It is long stretches of kelly green grape vines, the bottoms of which are shaded dark by the fruit growing along the trellises. As I look out at the tranquil vista, it makes me think of the reasons for change, both in my neighborhood and abroad. What necessitates the change from oak chaparral to wine grapes? What brings along the changes that one neighborhood may view as dramatic, but from a distance seem so mild and unimportant. What might be next? Where does the land across the street and in front of my home go from here? Buildings? Wider roads? Why did the winery up the road need or want to buy up all the land to its south along the cool coastal ridge? Progress and profits? Pressure from competition? And where is this competition? Down the road? Or in another country?

The textbook I used for my first few MBA seminars was my friend in my assertion against much of the triviality of *The World Is Flat,* by Thomas Friedman, a writer for the *New York Times*. After all, what does a newspaperman (regardless of his credentials and writing talent) know about international trade and the implementation and management of normal business? Without worrying too much about his text, allow me to summarize his assertion: globalization is occurring at an unprecedented rate and somewhat equally around the world (thus the phenomenon) due to the advent of communication structures, the movement of goods and services, and mostly because of technology ubiquity. Well, I tend to disagree with most of the points, but suffice it to say I tell my students that the world is flat *in places*—that for the fully economically developed world, where technology infrastructures are similar, where Internet and telephone penetration rates are high, where roads are good, ports well managed, fuel supplies ample, and distribution and currency systems stable and well established, the world is flat. For the rest, it is not. The world is flat in places.

I prefer to buy the economic view that globalization has been spurred on by economic growth founded upon the increase in foreign investment rather than trade, which for centuries had been the engine that drove the bus. Once countries received investment, that money was put into infrastructure—projects that created jobs and allowed for materials to be produced or marketed, domestically and especially internationally. This increase in trade then made countries interdependent, and this interdependence is essentially globalization as we know it.

Globalization—treating the world as an available market—instigates interdependence between economies, which plays out as firms wanting and needing to go global, not only for growth but for survival. Survival is indeed the next step Mr. Freidman locked on to, and in this regard has made a correct assessment. However, don't forget that the basis for his assertion—the need to be competitive and to survive—is not properly based; that is, in a world that is flat only in places. In other words, his argument is valid only for the connected markets—those flat markets I alluded to—along with developing markets that have made recent technology infrastructure investments.

In fact, this point is so important that I think the media glomming onto the Freidman efforts really has done a disservice to the worldwide discussion about globalization, its reasons, its importance, and its relevance. MBA programs tend to accept the reasoning as a pragmatic application of principles—in part, I think, because MBA programs, like most academic pursuits, are insulated from the actual business world. I suppose I peg myself into this category, but I hope that my dependence on critical thinking keeps my mind open to the counterarguments laid out in this chapter.

I remember, during my first job out of graduate school, our company's American CEO used to repeat that taking risk was important, and that to truly know success you had to experience failure. Or something like that. I had wondered whether he was speaking from personal experience or whether he told us those words to maintain our edge against a monolithic Japanese business culture. Based on my own history, I think that risk-taking—embracing measured risk—is crucially important in order to get a full international development experience. And having that experience later allows you to lead others into the fray.